THE WEAPONS ENCYCLOPÆDIA
TANK AIRCRAFT AFV SHIP ARTILLERY VEHICLES SECRET WEAPON

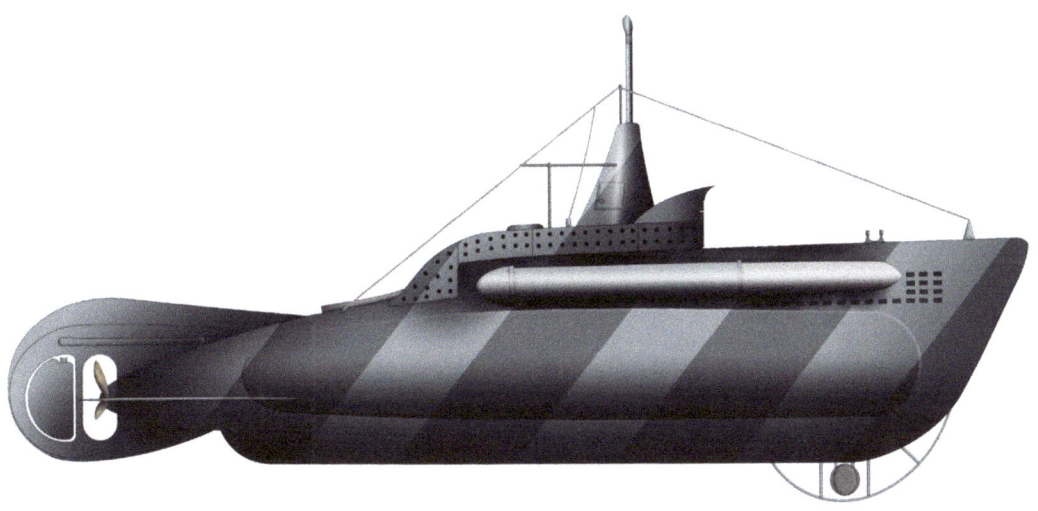

ITALIAN NAVY SPECIAL FORCES WWII

THE WEAPONS ENCYCLOPAEDIA

EDITORIAL STAFF
Luca Cristini, Paolo Crippa.

ACADEMIC STAFF
Enrico Acerbi, Massimiliano Afiero, Aldo Antonicelli, Ruggero Calò, Luigi Carretta, Flavio Chistè, Anna Cristini, Carlo Cucut, Salvo Fagone, Enrico Finazzer, Arturo Giusti, Björn Huber, Andrea Lombardi, Aymeric Lopez, Marco Lucchetti, Gabriele Malavoglia, Luigi Manes, Giovanni Maressi, Francesco Mattesini, Daniele Notaro, Péter Mujzer, Federico Peirani, Alberto Peruffo, Maurizio Raggi, Andrea Alberto Tallillo, Antonio Tallillo, Roberto Vela, Massimo Zorza.

PUBLISHED BY
Luca Cristini Editore (Soldiershop), via Orio, 35/4 - 24050 Zanica (BG) ITALY.

DISTRIBUTION BY
Soldiershop - www.soldiershop.com, Amazon, Ingram Spark, Berliner Zinnfigurem (D), LaFeltrinelli, Mondadori, Libera Editorial (Spain), Google book (eBook), Kobo, (eBoook), Apple Book (eBook).

PUBLISHING'S NOTES
None of unpublished images or text of our book may be reproduced in any format without the expressed written permission of Luca Cristini Editore (already Soldiershop.com) when not indicate as marked with license creative commons 3.0 or 4.0. Luca Cristini Editore has made every reasonable effort to locate, contact and acknowledge rights holders and to correctly apply terms and conditions to Content. Every effort has been made to trace the copyright of all the photographs. If there are unintentional omissions, please contact the publisher in writing at: info@soldiershop.com, who will correct all subsequent editions.

LICENSES COMMONS
This book may utilize part of material marked with license creative commons 3.0 or 4.0 (CC BY 4.0), (CC BY-ND 4.0), (CC BY-SA 4.0) or (CC0 1.0). We give appropriate attribution credit and indicate if change were made in the acknowledgments field. Our WTW books series utilize only fonts licensed under the SIL Open Font License or other free use license.

CONTRIBUTORS OF THIS VOLUME & ACKNOWLEDGEMENTS
We would like to thank the main contributors to this issue: The wagon profiles are all by the author. The colouring of the photos is by the author. Special thanks to national and/or private institutions such as: Army General Staff, State Archives, Bundesarchiv, Nara, Library of Congress, Wikipedia, USAF, Signal magazine, War Chronicles, War Front, IWM, Australian War Museum, etc. A P.Crippa, A.Lopez, Péter Mujzer, L.Manes, C.Cucut, Tallillo archives. Italeri, Model Victoria (www.modelvictoria.it) Italeri, etc. for making available pictures or anything else from their archives. Special thanks to all modellers, their clubs and modelling companies for the courtesy use of their images. As far as possible we will always include the names of the authors. Please let us know in case you have not been able to locate them.

For a complete list of Soldiershop titles, or for every information please contact us on our website: www.soldiershop.com or www.cristinieditore.com. E-mail: info@soldiershop.com. Keep up to date on Facebook https://www.facebook.com/soldiershop.publishing

Title: **Italian Navy special forces WWII** Code.: **TWE-038 EN**
Series by L. S. Cristini
ISBN code: 9791255892335 First edition May 2025
THE WEAPONS ENCYCLOPAEDIA (SOLDIERSHOP) is a trademark of Luca Cristini Editore

THE WEAPONS ENCYCLOPÆDIA
TANK AIRCRAFT AFV SHIP ARTILLERY VEHICLES SECRET WEAPON

ITALIAN NAVY SPECIAL FORCES WWII

THE ITALIAN *WUNDERWAFFEN*

LUCA STEFANO CRISTINI

BOOK SERIES FOR MODELERS & COLLECTORS

CONTENTS

Introduction .... pag. 5
   - The Navy and secret weapons .... pag. 7

Slow-moving torpedoes S.L.C. .... pag. 9

Assault boats and motorboats .... pag. 17

Midget submarines .... pag. 27

Class CM & CC submarines .... pag. 49

Special transport submarines .... pag. 53
   - The daring attack project in New York .... pag. 59

The secret bases of the assault vehicles .... pag. 61
   - The Montecolino (Iseo) base .... pag. 61
   - The Base of the Adige-Garda Tunnel .... pag. 65

Assault vehicles models .... pag. 67

Bibliography .... pag. 70

▲ The submarine *Gondar*, with the four SLC landing craft containers. On the later submarines *Scirè* and *Ambra*, equipped to force enemy ships, the containers were reduced to three, one at the bow and two at the stern of the turret.

INTRODUCTION

ITALIAN MILITARY POLICY BETWEEN MYTH AND REALITY: TECHNOLOGY AND INDUSTRIAL LIMITS

"We are a people of eight million bayonets," "Strength must first and foremost lie in numbers." These slogans, often evoked to summarize the fascist regime's military policy on the eve of World War II, became emblematic of the regime's apparent strategic backwardness in a conflict where technology and industrial power would play a decisive role.

However, like all historical simplifications, this one captures only part of the truth. While the regime glorified the numerical strength of Italians, it also sought to embody a modernist ambition, supported by scientific luminaries like Guglielmo Marconi and Enrico Fermi, and cutting-edge sectors such as the Air Force.

THE INDUSTRIAL GAP AND ITALY'S "WUNDERWAFFEN"

Despite these aspirations, fascist Italy had to contend with an industry that was structurally weaker and more backward than those of other European powers, unable to compete in terms of innovation, production, and wartime conversion. This did not, however, prevent the development of some advanced weapons, albeit with fewer resources and less success than Nazi Germany.

Among the most enigmatic projects was the so-called *"Death Ray,"* a directed-energy weapon akin to a laser, on which Marconi himself worked, intended to strike targets at great distances. A fascinating idea, but one that quickly faded into legend. Despite the difficulties, the Italian armed forces experimented with several ingenious solutions:

The Army with its 26-ton P40 tank, which remained in development due to the 1943 armistice; **the Air Force** with its: Reggiane Re.2005 *"Sagittario,"* one of Italy's best fighters, comparable to the Spitfire but produced in limited numbers due to material shortages; Piaggio P.108, Italy's only four-engine bomber, also deployed against Gibraltar; and above all, the Campini-Caproni C.C.2, Italy's first jet aircraft, making Italy the second country in the world, after Germany, to fly a jet.

▲ Specimen of the WWII "pig" (technical name: "slow-moving torpedo") on display in the Villa Comunale in Taormina. Photo by Edward Derelacourtesy Wiki CC.

▲ Major of Naval Engineers Teseo Tesei (1909 - 26 July 1941), died in combat action with one of his SLC pigs in Valletta, Malta. Gold Medal for Military Valour in his memory.

THE NAVY AND SECRET WEAPONS

It was the Regia Marina, however, that distinguished itself with the most innovative projects, many of which remain little-known to the public. Among these: the SLC (*Siluro a Lenta Corsa*), better known as the *"Maiale"* (Pig): an underwater assault craft protagonist of several daring missions. And the MTM (*Motoscafo d'Assalto*), or explosive motorboat: small vessels piloted by volunteers, similar to the Japanese *Kaiten*.

Finally, the mini-submarines, where Italians were pioneers; some of these were even intended to attack New York Harbor in 1943—a project still shrouded in mystery today.

This book aims to explore these lesser-known pages of Italian military history, revealing how, despite structural limitations, the fascist regime attempted to compete in the field of wartime innovation.

But why did Italy's "miracle weapons" fail? Primarily due to resource scarcity: Italy lacked the industrial capacity of Germany or the U.S. Delays in development, also for economic reasons, meant many projects arrived too late. Italy's *"Wunderwaffen"* were often ingenious but rarely decisive, unlike their German counterparts (such as the V1 and V2). Yet, vehicles like the SLC (*Maiali*) demonstrated the effectiveness of Italy's asymmetric warfare.

▲ CB1 type mini-submarine named *"Malibran"* stored in Zagreb (Croatia).

SLC "PIG" ASSAULT TORPEDOES AND "MIGNATTA" TORPEDOES 1918-1945

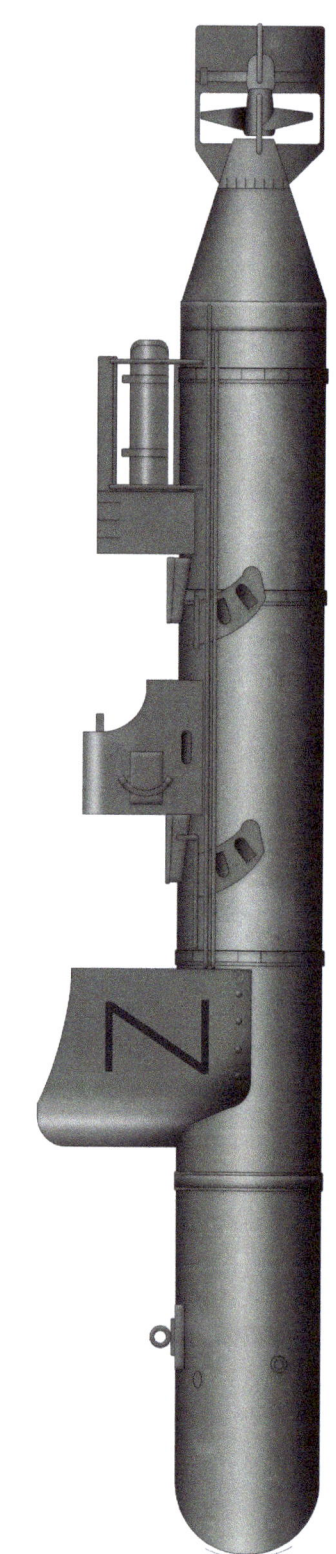

▲ One of the best known of the Navy's assault units, the pigs, or rather the SLC slow-moving torpedoes, were special vehicles that covered themselves in glory during the Second World War. Their most famous action was the raid on the port of Alexandria. Above: the classic SLC model. Below: the Rossetti self-propelled torpedo boat, also known as the Mignatta.

SLOW-RUNNING TORPEDOES S.L.C.

■ IN THE BEGINNING, THERE WAS THE "MIGNATTA"

The Rossetti self-propelled torpedine, better known by its nickname *"Mignatta"* (Leech), represented one of the most ingenious innovations in underwater assault weapons developed during World War I. Designed by naval engineer Raffaele Rossetti, an officer of the Italian Naval Engineers, this unique weapon was conceived for sabotage operations against enemy ships anchored in harbors. Its most famous use occurred during the *Impresa di Pola* (November 1, 1918), when it was deployed to sink the Austro-Hungarian battleship SMS *Viribus Unitis*, marking one of the Italian Navy's boldest feats in the conflict.

Technical Specifications and Operation
The *Mignatta*, 8 meters long and 600 mm in diameter, was derived from a modified French Schneider torpedo model A.115/450. Unlike conventional torpedoes, it was designed to carry two operators, initially seated astride the hull. However, during operational tests, it proved more effective for the men to slide along the sides, gripping handles fixed to the cylinder. Propulsion was provided by compressed air stored in a central tank, powering two four-bladed propellers, allowing a range of 10 nautical miles at a speed of 2 knots. Lacking a rudder, directional control relied on the physical strength of the operators, who adjusted the trajectory by extending their arms and legs to steer the craft.

Armament and Sabotage Techniques
The forward section housed two explosive charges of 175 kg each, detachable and equipped with clockwork fuses to trigger detonation. Originally designed to attach to enemy hulls via electromagnetic clamps (hence the nickname *"Mignatta,"* for its leech-like adherence), the charges were secured with ropes during the *Viribus Unitis* mission due to docking difficulties. The device also included a self-destruct mechanism in the aft section, consisting of a timed charge activatable to prevent capture.

Evolution and Historical Impact
Rossetti's design laid the groundwork for the development of future slow-running torpedoes (SLC), known as *"Maiali,"* successfully employed during World War II. However, research in this field slowed abruptly in the 1930s due to Rossetti's anti-fascist activism, which in 1936 cost him the revocation of his Gold Medal of Military Valor—an unprecedented measure. Only later did the Italian Navy vigorously resume the development of assault craft and special forces, direct heirs to Rossetti's daring invention. The *Impresa di Pola* and the *Mignatta* remain the baptism of fire for Italian naval operations, heralding a new era in underwater warfare.

▲ Beautiful model of the Mignata-Rossetti from the Militia Models Italian Kit line in 1.35 resin. Courtesy.

SLC MODEL 227 "PIGS" ASSAULT TORPEDOES, ITALY-LIGURIA 1942-1945

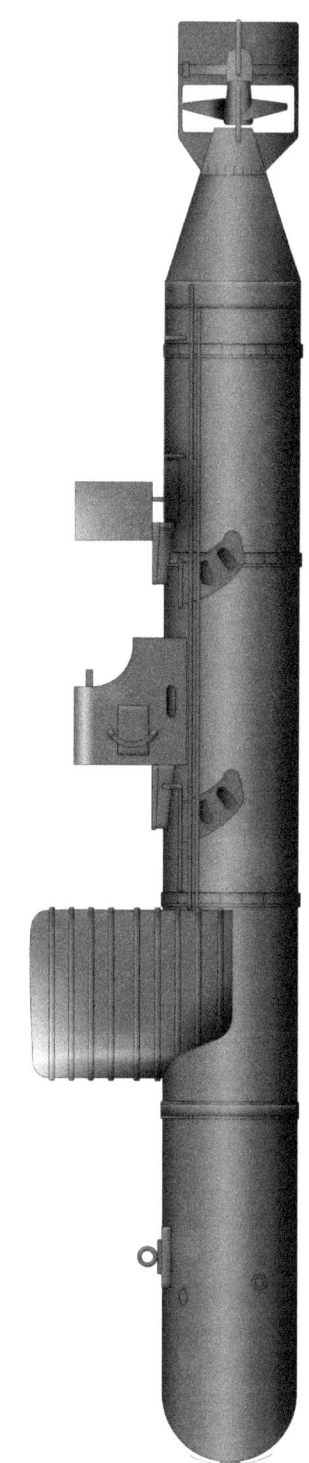
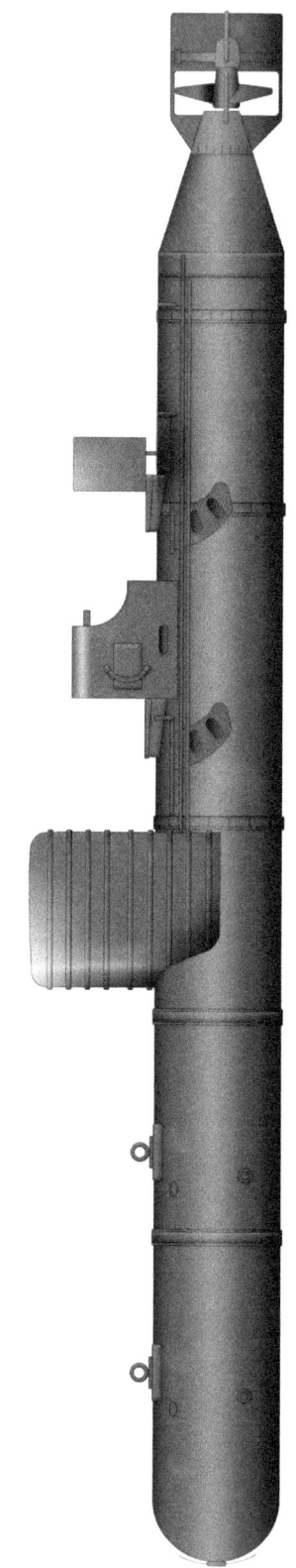

◂ Specimen SLC nr 227, avant-garde type, created in two versions: normal and evolved (basically with a larger charge and thus a longer torpedo). Model used by the 10th Mas flotilla at Bocca di Serchio, 1942.

THE «MAIALE»: THE MOST FAMOUS SLC TORPEDO

The idea of an evolution of Rossetti's modified torpedo from World War I took shape thanks to the ingenuity of two officers of the Naval Engineers Corps: Teseo Tesei and Elios Toschi, both experts in submarine machinery. Their design envisioned a low-speed underwater craft piloted by two operators equipped with autonomous breathing apparatuses, capable of transporting an explosive charge to be covertly attached to enemy hulls.

The nickname *"Maiale"* (Pig) was adopted as a codename by Tesei to protect the secrecy of the craft.

In 1939, the Navy unit training in SLC use was relocated to a secret base at Bocca di Serchio; it was on this river and the adjacent coastal waters that repeated training trials refined the weapon to perfection.

The Regia Marina's General Staff authorized the construction of a first prototype in early 1935 at the San Bartolomeo Torpedo Workshop in La Spezia. In reality, two units were built, using recycled materials wherever possible. The first prototype, completed in November 1935, delivered mediocre but encouraging results. The second, tested in 1936, revealed further issues, gradually resolved through subsequent modifications.

To this day, the exact number of units produced remains uncertain, but estimates suggest no more than 45–50, divided as follows:

- 1st prototype (1935)
- 2nd prototype (1936)
- 1st Series (1936): 4 units
- 2nd Series (1939): 5 units
- "100" Series (1940): 8 units
- "200" Series (1941–1943): 24–30 units

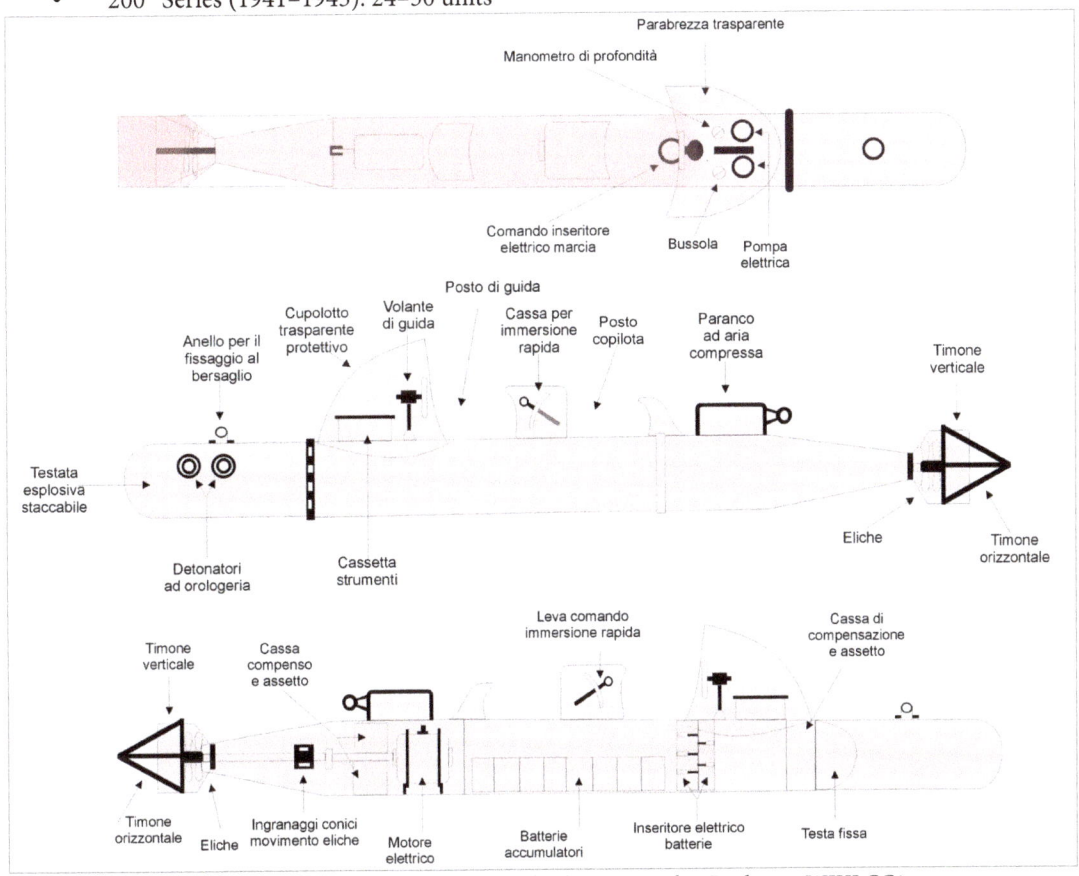

▲ Complete diagram of the SLC Slow-running torpedo (pig). Courtesy by Guidomac WIKI CC1.

ASSAULT TORPEDOES SLC SAN BARTOLOMEO, ITALY 1940-1945

▲ The most advanced slow-moving torpedo was the so-called St Bartholomew's version.

ITALIAN NAVY SPECIAL FORCES WWII

■ TECHNICAL SPECIFICATIONS AND OPERATIONAL USE

The S.L.C., conceptually derived from Rossetti and Paolucci's *"Mignatta"* (1918), became the most famous underwater assault craft of the Xª Flottiglia MAS, achieving significant results throughout World War II. The craft was equipped with:

- A 260 kg explosive charge of Tritolite or Tritolital, positioned in the bow.
- A 1.6 HP electric motor, initially connected to two counter-rotating coaxial propellers, later replaced by a single 38 cm propeller to reduce noise.
- A 30-cell battery pack delivering 180 A at 60 V, providing a theoretical range of 15 nautical miles at 2.3 knots (with a maximum submerged speed of 3 knots).
- Rapid diving capability, reaching operational depth in just 7 seconds.

On December 19, 1941, the *"Maiali"* SLCs deployed by the Xª Flottiglia MAS executed their most celebrated mission: the sinking of the British battleships HMS *Valiant* and HMS *Queen Elizabeth* and the damaging of a tanker and a destroyer in Alexandria's harbor. The three assault craft had been transported near the enemy base by the submarine *Scirè*, each *"Maiale"* housed in specialized cylinders on the deck. However, the Italians also used the interned ship *Olterra* in Algeciras (Spain) as an operational base, from which both «*Maiali*» and Gamma divers launched attacks against the nearby British base.

■ THE DELTA ASSAULT CRAFT – THE SAN BARTOLOMEO TORPEDO (S.S.B.)

The operational use of the classic S.L.C. (*Maiali*) revealed certain limitations, while technological progress suggested the need for a more advanced craft. On the initiative of Major Mario Masciulli of the Naval Engineers, with the collaboration of Captain G.N. Travaglini (responsible for the secret workshop on the tanker *Olterra*, interned in Algeciras near Gibraltar) and the consultancy of engineer Guido Cattaneo of C.A.B.I. in Milan, a new model was developed: the *Siluro San Bartolomeo* (S.S.B.), officially designated the *Tipo Delta*.

Improvements and Features

Compared to the S.L.C., the S.S.B. featured:
- A broader upper casing, better protecting the operators;
- Larger dimensions: diameter increased from 0.553 m to 0.780 m, with unchanged length (6.766 m);

▲ A slow-moving torpedo (SL.), known as "pig", operated by its inventor Teseo Tesei.

- Enhanced explosive charge of 400 kg;
- A 7.5 HP electric motor, powered by two battery packs (190 Ah at 60 V), connected to two counter-rotating three-bladed propellers;
- Superior performance: submerged speed of 4.5 knots and surfaced speed of 2.5 knots, with a range of 15 nautical miles at reduced speed.

Despite these advances, the armistice of September 8, 1943, prevented mass production. Only a few prototypes were completed, including:

- Two units remaining in La Spezia, assigned to the *"Gruppo Operativo della Castagna"* (commanded by Lieutenant Augusto Jacobacci);
- One unit sent to Venice, recovered at the end of the war.

The S.S.B. represented a promising evolution, but the deteriorating war situation prevented its operational use, relegating it to an unfinished chapter in the history of Italian assault craft.

▲ Classic SLC 'pig' piece, currently on display at the Shrine of Armed Forces Flags at the Victor Emmanuel II monument in Rome. Courtesy by Myrabella Wiki CC1.

▲ World War II "pig" of the type known as the "St Bartholomew Torpedo", currently on display at the Submarine Museum in Gosportm (UK). Wiki CC1.

▲▼ Four pictures of a slow-moving torpedo presented at the well-known Italian "Militaria" exhibition at the eposizioni park in Novegro (MI), photo by Luca Cristini.

S.L.C. DATA SHEET		
Model	SLC Maiale	SLC San Bartolomeo
Producer	Officina Siluri San Bartolomeo di La Spezia	
Crew	2	2
Entry and exit from service	1935-1945	1943-1945
Weight	1800 kg	2200 kg
Engine	Electric motor 1.1 to 1.6 HP	Electric motor 7.5 hp
Maximum speed	3 knots (2,3 underwater)	4 knots
Autonomy	15 nautical miles	10 nautical miles
Engine battery power	150 Ampere - 60 volts	190 Ampere - 60 volts
Armament	Explosive head 260 kg	Explosive head 300 kg
Secondary armament	-	Explosive head 400 kg
Production	45/50 pieces	3 pieces
Length-Width-Height	6,7-0,53-1,0 m	6,77-0,79-1.08 m

▲ From top: reconstructed SLC piece on display at the Taranto Arsenal Historical Exhibition. By robertoorlando wiki cc1. Below: another view of the slow-running torpedo presented at the well-known Italian "Militaria" exhibition at the epsosizioni park in Novegro (MI), photo by Luca Cristini.

EXPLOSIVE MOTORBOATS AND ASSAULT CRAFT

EXPLOSIVE MOTORBOATS: THE DARING ASSAULT CRAFT OF THE REGIA MARINA

In the naval history of World War II, explosive motorboats represent one of the boldest and most ingenious solutions employed by the Italian Regia Marina. Developed starting in 1935, these assault motorboats, known as M.T.M. (*Motoscafo Turismo Modificato*) and M.T.S. (*Motoscafo Turismo Silurante*), were produced in about a hundred units, distinguishing themselves in some of the conflict's riskiest operations.

A Weapon of Strategic Impact
Though not all missions were successful, explosive motorboats wrote memorable chapters in history. The most famous feat occurred on the night of March 25–26, 1941, when six of these craft, led by Lieutenant Luigi Faggioni, penetrated Suda Bay in Crete, sinking the British cruiser HMS *York* and the 8,000-ton tanker *Pericles*. A resounding success, demonstrating the potential of these small but deadly vessels.
Other operations, however, ended in tragedy, such as the failed attack on Malta in April 1941, which cost the lives of 18 sailors and assault divers of the X MAS. Despite setbacks, explosive motorboats were used until the war's final days, as seen in the action by Petty Officer Sergio Denti against the French destroyer *Trombe*, just before Italy's surrender.

Technology and Tactics: How the Motorboats Operated
These craft combined simplicity with lethal precision. The pilot, positioned at the stern on a cantilevered seat, steered the boat toward the target at maximum speed before abandoning it at the last moment. The 300 kg explosive charge, containing Tritolital, was placed in the bow and triggered on impact with the enemy hull, detonating underwater to maximize damage.
The torpedo-equipped variants, larger and more powerful, were armed with a 450 mm torpedo and two 70 kg depth charges, expanding attack options.

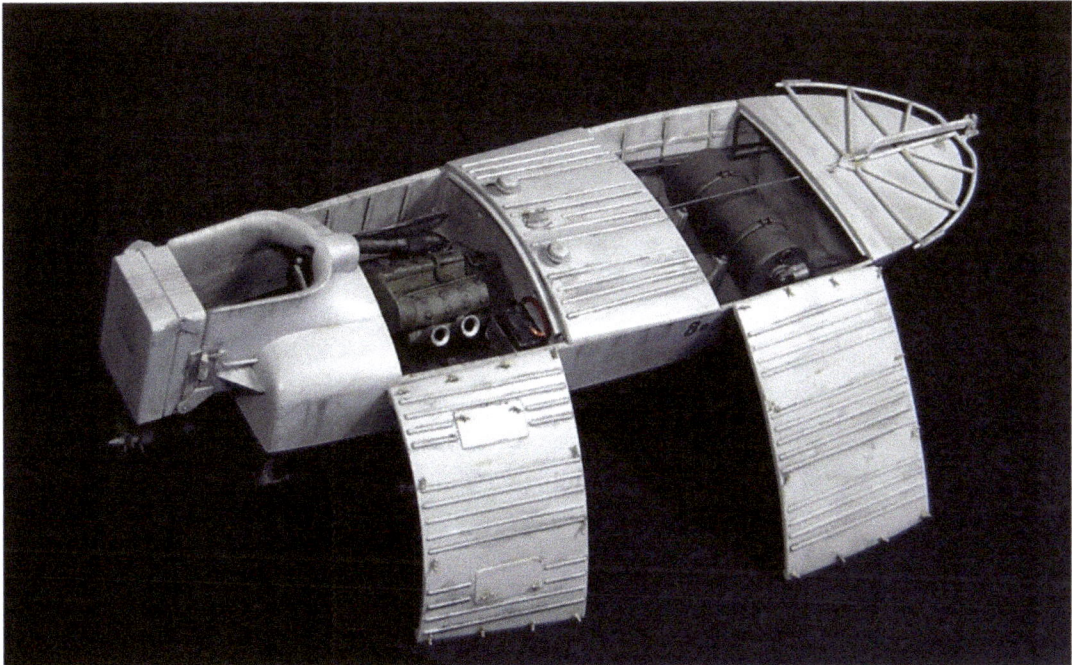

▲ An "open" view of the explosive boat, made from the Italeri kit by Leonardo Thunderjet F. model maker.

MAIN VARIANTS AND EVOLUTION

Throughout the war, the Regia Marina developed several versions of explosive motorboats, each optimized for specific operational needs:
- M.T.M. (*Motoscafo Turismo Modificato*) – 1.2 tons, 90 HP, 31 knots (1935–1940)
- M.T.R. (*Motoscafo Turismo Ridotto*) – Designed for submarine transport.
- M.A.T. (*Motoscafo Avio Trasportato*) – Designed for aerial transport.
- M.T.S. (*Motoscafo Turismo Silurante*) – 1.75 tons, 90 HP, 28 knots (1940–1941)
- M.T.S.M. (*Motoscafo Turismo Silurante Modificato*) – 3 tons, 190 HP, 32 knots (1941–1945)
- M.T.S.M.A. (*Motoscafo Turismo Silurante Modificato Allargato*) – 3.7 tons, 190 HP, 29 knots (1943–1945)
- M.T.L. (*Motoscafo Trasporto Lento*) – Used to transport *Maiali* to operational zones (1941–1945)

A Legacy Beyond Borders

The idea of explosive motorboats was not confined to Italy. Germany and Japan developed similar craft: the Germans with *Linsen*, the Japanese with *Shinyo*, the latter designed for suicide missions. Meanwhile, the Decima MAS also deployed the famous *"Maiali,"* the Slow-Running Torpedoes (SLC), protagonists of the legendary attack on Alexandria Bay in 1941, while the Japanese used the lethal *Kaiten*, high-speed piloted torpedoes. Today, explosive motorboats remain a symbol of military courage and ingenuity, a testament to how small craft, guided by determined men, could threaten even the mightiest warships.

THE EXPLOSIVE MOTORBOAT: A LETHAL AND SILENT WEAPON

The operational base for explosive motorboats was located in La Spezia, particularly at the Balipedio Cottrau, where these small but deadly craft were prepared for their most daring missions. Built with lightweight hulls and gasoline engines derived from racing models, the motorboats combined agility and power, reaching high speeds that—coupled with their low profile—made them difficult to detect, especially at night or dawn. Their primary weapon was a 300 kg explosive charge placed in the bow. Upon impact with the enemy hull, the motorboat would sink several meters, allowing a hydrostatic device to trigger detonation. The explosion, amplified by water pressure, caused devastating damage to the target's hull, often compromising its structural integrity irreparably. The pilot, after aiming at the target, would abandon the craft at about 80 meters, throwing himself backward onto a specially designed backrest that doubled as a life raft, shielding him from the blast wave.

▲ Example of the explosive MTM (Modified Touring Motorboat), housed in the Naval Museum, Haifa, Israel. Courtesy by Bukvoed Wiki CC1.

M.T.M EXPLOSIVE BOAT, ITALY 1940-1945

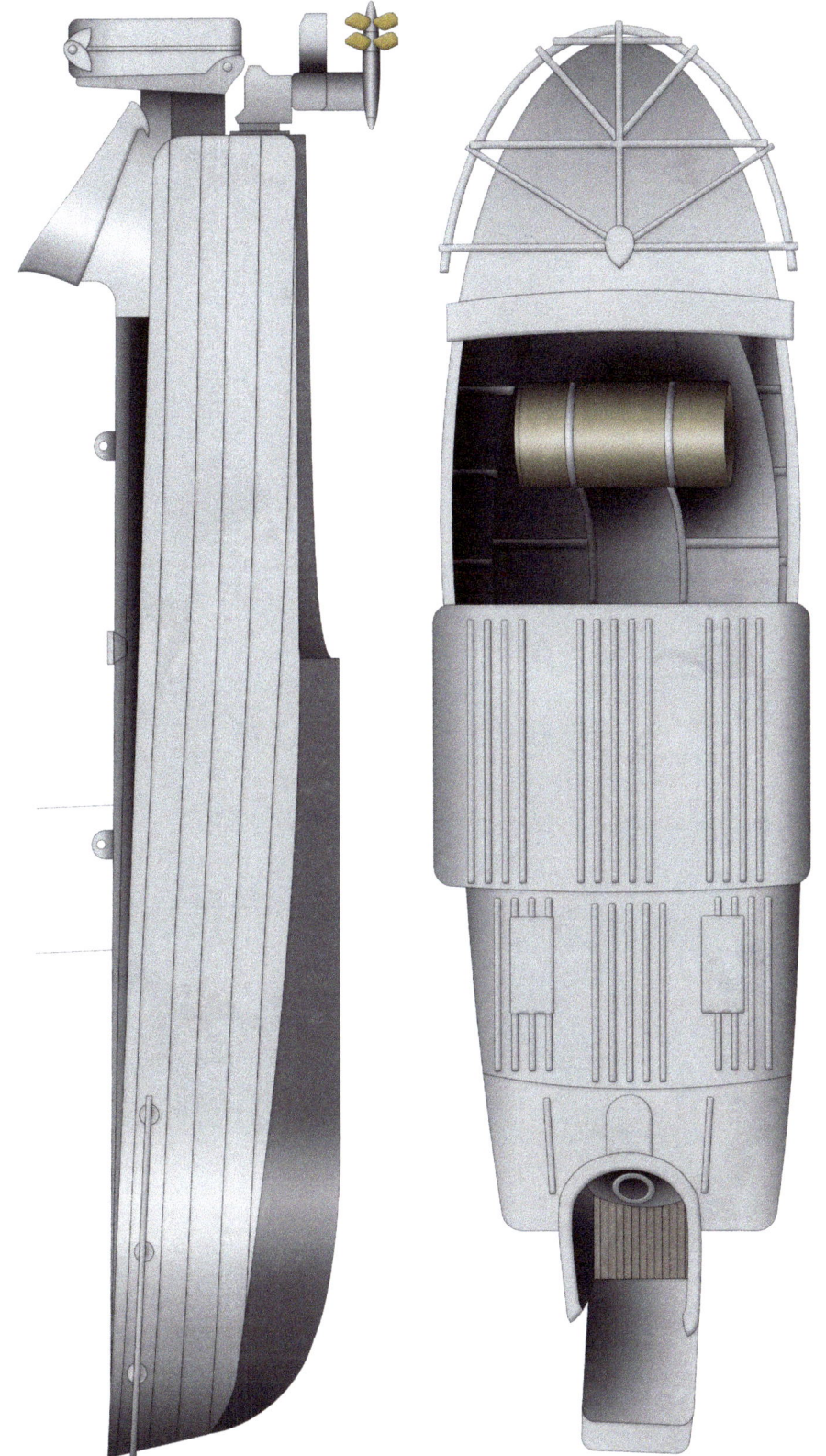

▲ The explosive boat represented a series of assault motorboats developed by the Regia Marina since 1935.

M.T.S.M MODIFIED EXPLOSIVE BOAT, ITALY 1941-1945

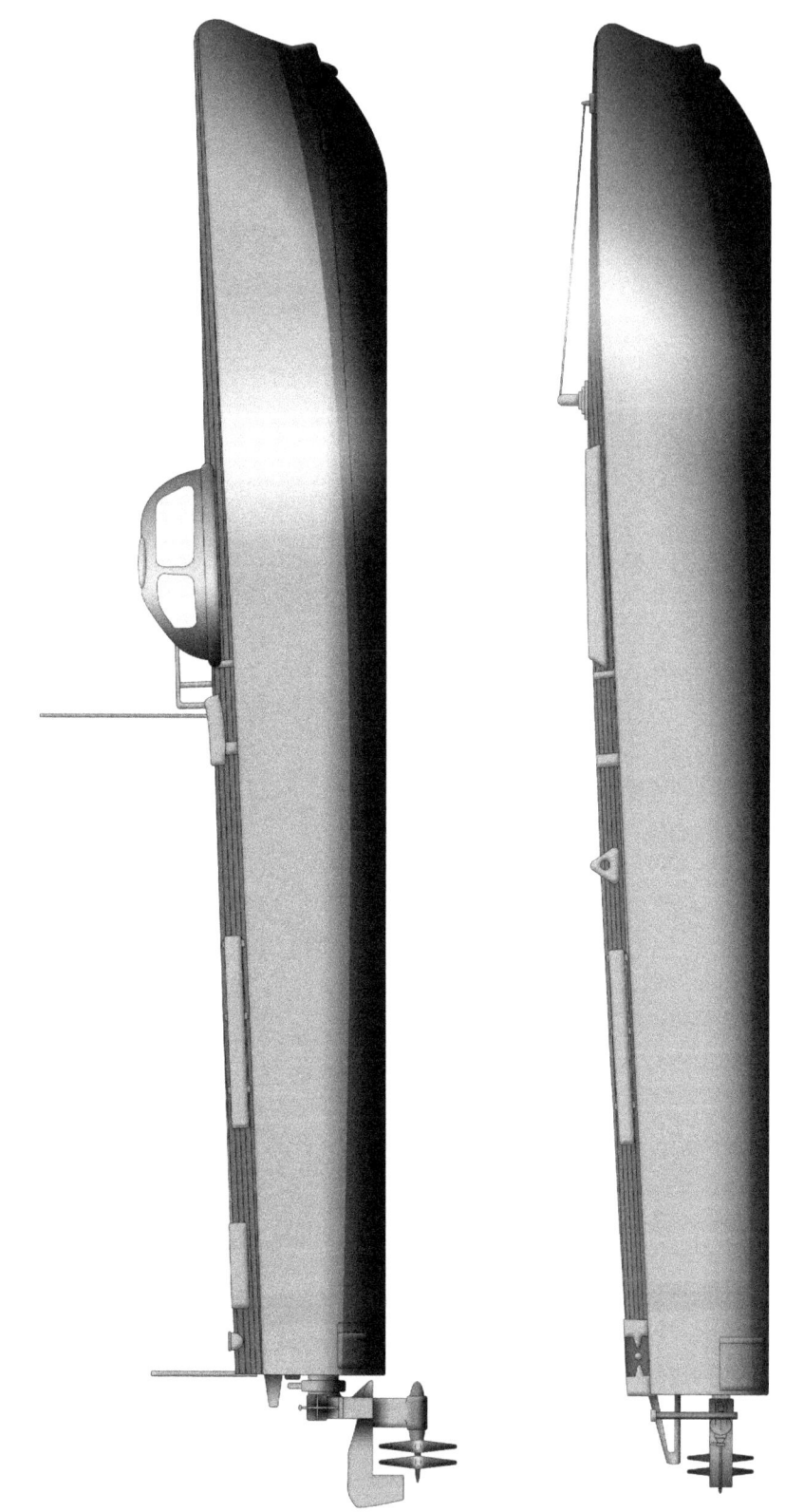

▲ The explosive boat developed by the Regia Marina from 1935 onwards in 7/8 variants and sizes.

1) The M.T.M. (*Motoscafo Turismo Modificato*): The Standard Assault Craft

Affectionately nicknamed *"emme"* by Decima MAS operators, the M.T.M. became, by late 1941, the flotilla's standard explosive motorboat and the most widely produced model.

Armament:
- Explosive charge: 300–350 kg of Tritolital (an enhanced variant of TNT), contained in a large cylinder in the bow.
- Attack method: After locking the rudder, the pilot would ram the craft into the enemy ship before throwing himself into the water onto a small lifebuoy. The charge, penetrating deep, would explode with devastating effect.

2) The M.T.R. (*Motoscafo Turismo Ridotto*): Versatility and Submarine Transport

Designed in 1942, the M.T.R. aimed to reduce size and weight compared to the M.T.M., making it transportable via submarines in watertight containers.

Technical Specifications:
- Displacement: 1 ton
- Dimensions: 6.11 m long, 30 cm narrower than the M.T.M.
- Speed: 29 knots (thanks to the same 95 HP engine as earlier models)
- Range: 80 nautical miles

A first series of 8 units was delivered in October 1942, followed by a second series of 12 slightly modified units (M.T.R.M.) by September 1943. Despite their potential, these craft saw limited use, with only one attempted attack on Syracuse. After the armistice, four units were assigned to the Italian Social Republic (R.S.I.).

3) The M.T.S. (*Motoscafo Turismo Silurante*): The "Omega Project"

Approved in January 1941, the M.T.S. (also referred to as the *"Omega Project"*) represented an evolution toward a multirole craft capable of torpedo attacks.

Features:
- Hull: Wooden, low-vee hull
- Dimensions: 6.5 m (length) × 2.2 m (width) × 1.75 m (height)
- Armament: Two 450 mm torpedoes, shortened to 3.2 meters and launched astern via pneumatic pistons.

4) The M.T.S.M. (*Motoscafo Turismo Silurante Modificato*): Enhanced Version

An improvement on the M.T.S., this variant introduced:
- A lengthened hull

▲ Left: a picture of the MTSMA model (the modified enlarged torpedo touring boat) that also operated in the Black Sea. Right image: two reduced-looking MTMs, could be MTRs.

- A redesigned hull for greater stability
- Reduction to a single torpedo
- Twin engines for increased power and reliability

5) The M.T.S.M.A. (*Motoscafo Turismo Silurante Modificato Allargato*): The Final Evolution
The last development in the series, the M.T.S.M.A., featured:
- Increased dimensions (8.77 m long)
- Armament: One torpedo, depth charges, and smoke generators for diversified missions.

6) The M.A.T. (*Motoscafo Avio Trasportato*): Aerial Transport
The M.A.T. was a motorboat used by the Regia Marina during World War II for assault and raiding operations, designed to be transported by aircraft. Essentially an evolution of the various Assault Motorboats (M.A.), it was equipped with a bow-mounted explosive charge and transported to the operational zone via a seaplane, suspended from the aircraft's floats.

The M.A.T. was transported to the operational zone by a seaplane, particularly the SIAI S.55.

7) The M.T.L. (*Motoscafo Trasporto Lento per SLC*): The "Maiale" Carrier

The *"Motoscafo Trasporto Lento per SLC"* was a motorboat used to transport and deploy Slow-Running Torpedoes (SLC) near target ships, allowing sailors to position the underwater torpedo and approach undetected. Colonel G.N. Mizzau studied and designed several models of SLC transport boats, with a total of eleven units produced in three series. These motorboats were in service starting in spring 1941 as approach vessels for SLCs, whose maximum speed, recall, was 3 knots, with a range of about 15 nautical miles at 2.5 knots, according to the Navy. Hence the tactical importance of a fast «approach craft.»

Conclusion: A Legacy of Ingenuity and Courage
Explosive motorboats and their derivatives represent a fascinating chapter in Italian naval history, where technology, tactics, and audacity merged into vessels that, despite their small size, threatened far more powerful ships. Their evolution reflects continuous adaptation to wartime needs, leaving an indelible mark on the operations of the Decima Flottiglia MAS.

▲ Due belle immagini del barchino espolsivo MTM. Colorazione dell'autore.

M.T.L MOTORBOAT SLOW TRANSPORT 1ST SERIES, ITALY 1941-1945

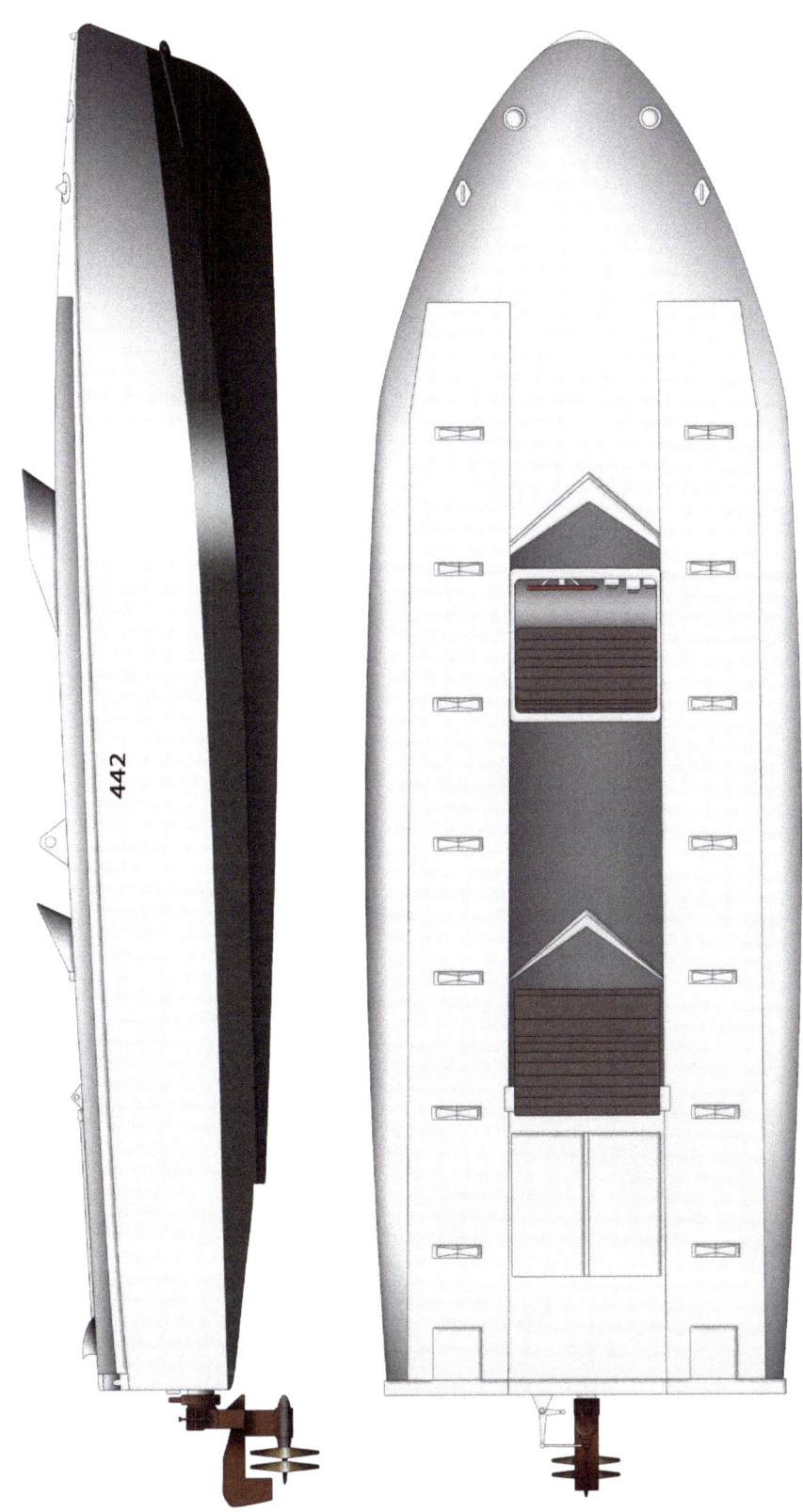

▲ The M.T.L. slow transport boat was a vehicle designed to bring one or two S.L.C. pigs close to the target.

ITALIAN NAVY SPECIAL FORCES WWII

▲▼ Several pictures of the MTM explosive boat preserved at the naval museum in La Spezia.

THE 'R' BOAT (RAMOGNINO)

The "Gamma" system and the innovation of the "R" boat: it was an ingenious solution but with several limitations to overcome. From the earliest trials, the weapon system represented by the "Gamma" operators showed potential, but also revealed a critical inherent limitation: the reduced range and low speed in the water, which were solely tied to the physical capabilities of the operator. The swimmer-swimmer, in fact, was forced to personally haul the explosive charges: tapered but heavy trunks, which greatly hampered their operational effectiveness. It therefore became necessary to study and introduce an individual vehicle capable of efficient transportation without compromising stealth, especially in the final stages of approaching the target. The solution emerged thanks to the intuition of officer and engineer Antonio Ramognino, a former X MAS agent, who in 1941 merged his experience as a skilled canoeist with the technical skills gained at Piaggio's aeronautical factory. With the support of specialised workers, Ramognino designed a lightweight hull, similar to a "sandolin", characterised by a high elongation (length-to-width ratio) and propelled by paddle. Built in the Pontedera workshops, the boat used modern aeronautical aluminium alloys: Avional, Peraluman and Alume, guaranteeing lightness (around 70 kg) and resistance to support. Its dimensions, 4/5 m long and just 20 cm wide, optimised hydrodynamics and manoeuvrability, making it easier to overcome enemy harbour obstructions. The Gamma operator, lying on the hull, could thus carry explosive charges more efficiently, exploiting buoyancy. However, the Regia Marina requested further improvements, including the integration of a silent thruster. The addition of a Siemens electric motor (12,000 rpm, 1/8 reduction) and two pneumatic side pockets increased stability, but increased the weight to 250 kg. Despite this, the range was greatly enhanced and reached 35 miles at 4 knots, with a

load capacity of up to 350 kg of explosives. The first tests carried out at the Cottrau Balipedio (1942) were successful, leading to the production of a first series of "R" boats. However, Ramognino's urgent transfer to Spain, where he contributed greatly to the creation of secret bases such as Villa Carmela and Nave Olterra, together with some technical difficulties slowed down the "R" boat project. At the beginning of 1943, only six pieces were delivered to the X MAS Command, but their trace was lost for good before the armistice of 8 September. A promising idea, which remained unfinished due to wartime contingencies, but which represented a significant step forward in the evolution of special submarine operations.

▲ Profile of the boat "R", named after its inventor, engineer Antonio Ramognino, a former Piaggio technician, who became very famous, together with his wife, for the secret base of Villa Carmela in Algeciras, opposite Gibraltar. Pictured: engineer Antonio Ramognino wearing the uniform of the Regia Marina and his wife Conchita.

ITALIAN NAVY SPECIAL FORCES WWII

▲▼ Two beautiful images taken inside the workshop where the "R" boats were assembled, which allow us to see the good construction technique of the modern vehicles studied by Ramognino. Author colouring, page from Ass Naz. Arditi.

MIDGET SUBMARINES

■ MIDGET SUBMARINES: ORIGINS AND DEVELOPMENT OF A STRATEGIC WEAPON

Midget submarines, or mini-submarines, represent one of the most ingenious solutions in modern naval warfare. These compact underwater vessels, designed to accommodate minimal crews (2–3 men), could inflict disproportionate damage relative to their size. Though their use became widespread in the 20th century, the first prototypes date back as far as 1776.

With the evolution of traditional submarines—ever larger and more powerful—the need arose for tiny units capable of infiltrating enemy defenses and striking targets within harbors. This operational philosophy later expanded into multiple roles, proving that, despite their small size and low cost, mini-submarines could play a strategically pivotal role.

Deployment in World War II

Italy produced mini-submarines as early as World War I, including the Class B, rail-transportable type, laid down in 1915 in a batch of six, with only three units completed. These saw intensive service in coastal ambushes and close surveillance but did not participate in combat actions. During World War II, nearly all major navies experimented with Midget submarines or assault diver units. France's absence is explained by its 1940 capitulation, while the U.S., with its overwhelmingly superior conventional fleet, saw no need for such craft. More surprising was the absence of the USSR, despite Russia's engineering tradition in submarines.

■ THE CAPRONI CA: ITALY'S AMBITIOUS EXPERIMENT

In the late 1930s, fascist Italy began developing a new generation of Midget submarines for daring special operations along enemy coasts. The CA class, designed by Caproni under naval engineer Vincenzo Goeta's supervision, represented a pioneering attempt to create a compact yet lethal underwater weapon. Among the era's most intriguing projects were the Caproni CA Midget submarines, developed in 1937. Initially conceived for ambushes in narrow straits or infiltrating enemy bases, they proved ineffective, requiring a radical redesign that led to the CB class.

▲ Navigation trials with CA boat No. 2 in the waters of Lake Iseo, where Caproni had installed a secret base for the development of such weapons. In the background, the profile of Montisola could be seen in the morning mist.

CLASS B1 MIDGET SUBMARINE, ITALY 1915-16

▲ Midget submarine Class B1 of 1915, transportable by rail and intended for port surveillance, equipped with a single propeller driven by an internal combustion engine and electric motor. Speeds were 6.9 knots on the surface and 5 knots underwater. It was armed with two 450 mm torpedo tubes. Its measurements were: 15 m long, 2.5 wide and high. With a weight of 40 tons and a crew of 4 men.

The CA submarines, built by Caproni in Milan-Taliedo, featured an octagonal-section pressure hull, unpressurized double bottoms, and external torpedo tubes. Batteries were housed in a lower double bottom—an innovative but problematic solution.

The first two prototypes (CA1 and CA2) were completed in 1938. However, tests conducted in Venice and La Spezia revealed severe flaws: poor stability in rough seas, difficulty maintaining periscope depth, and an inefficient torpedo launch system. Excessive rolling and pitching also made life aboard nearly impossible. Consequently, the two boats were temporarily shelved.

Conversion into Assault Craft

With the outbreak of war, the Navy High Command considered converting the CAs into carriers for underwater assault teams. In 1941, the two prototypes were modified:
- The diesel engine was replaced with an electric motor.
- The periscope and torpedoes were removed, and a watertight keel hatch was added for diver deployment.
- The explosive payload was increased to eight 100 kg charges, transportable by operators.

The periscope was replaced with a cockpit and dome, while eight 100 kg charges took the place of torpedoes. Dimensions remained compact (10.47 m long, 1.90 m wide), with a displacement of 12.8 tons surfaced and 14 tons submerged. Maximum speed reached 7 knots surfaced and 6 knots submerged, with a submerged range limited to 57 nautical miles.

Tests on Lake Iseo, near Montecolino, where the project was advanced, highlighted the units' fragility, requiring constant adjustments. Nevertheless, in 1942, the Regia Marina ordered two more units (CA3 and CA4), with hull and charge placement modifications. The General Staff envisioned using these craft in high-profile missions, even attacking New York Harbor to bring the war to America's doorstep.

Plans called for deploying the CAs against U.S. ports, transported there by modified ocean-going submarines. In July 1942, CA2 was sent to Bordeaux to be loaded onto the submarine *Da Vinci*, but the operation was canceled due to shifting priorities. The unit remained unused until the war's end, when it

▲ Italy was already at the forefront with the First World War in the field of mini-submarines. Here in this Navy photo, the 1915 Class B1, doyen of the later CA and CB class midget submarines.

CAPRONI CLASS CA-1 MIDGET SUBMARINE, ITALY 1937-43

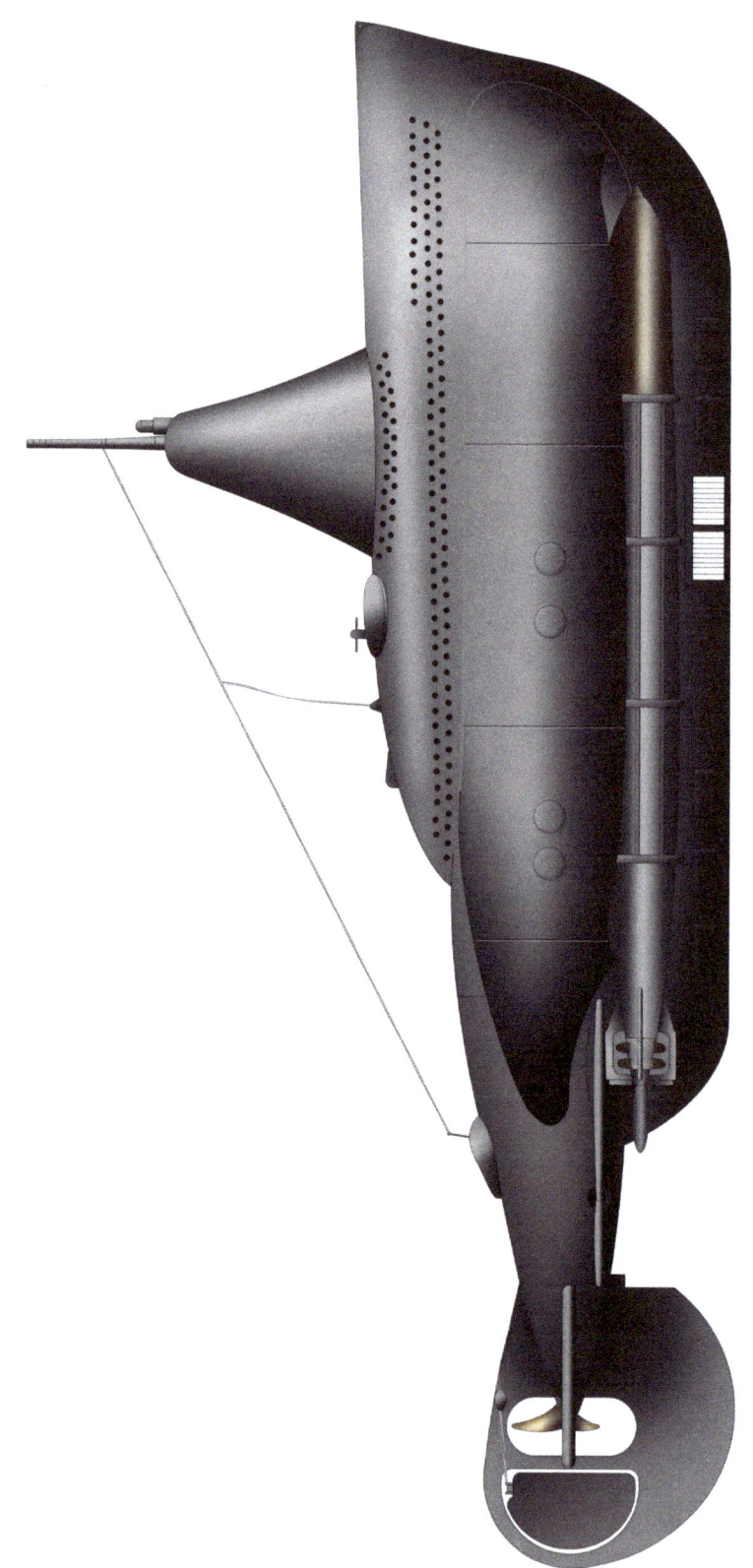

▲ Class CA model 1 midget submarine. It was on this model that the most severe tests were carried out at the Iseo secret base. It was determined that navalisation was very arduous and various arrangements were made to bring the boat into use for sabotage purposes. Thus, the Inaciasiluri tubes and the periscope were cut.

was scrapped. CA1, along with the second-series units, was scuttled in La Spezia on September 8, 1943, and later recovered. One unit, left in Bordeaux, fell into German hands, who studied it to develop their own Midget submarines.

As for those remaining in La Spezia, though the Republican National Navy considered their use, none ever saw active service. All were scrapped postwar, leaving a technological legacy that influenced later developments in underwater assault craft.

Technical Specifications
- CA Class (1st series, modified)
    - Displacement: 13.5 t (surfaced) / 16.4 t (submerged)
    - Dimensions: 10.00 × 1.96 × 1.60 m
    - Propulsion: Marelli electric motor (25 HP)
    - Speed: 6.25 knots (surfaced) / 5 knots (submerged)
    - Armament: 8 × 100 kg charges + 20 "bugs"
    - Crew: 1 officer + 1 petty officer
- CA Class (2nd series)
    - Displacement: 12.8 t (surfaced) / 14 t (submerged)
    - Dimensions: 10.47 × 1.90 × 1.83 m
    - Max depth: 70 m
    - Speed: 7 knots (surfaced) / 6 knots (submerged)

Conclusion: A Failed but Prophetic Experiment
The Caproni CAs were a bold experiment, marred by technical issues and operational misfortune. Though never deployed in action, they demonstrated the potential of mini-submarines as stealthy weapons, anticipating developments that would characterize postwar naval warfare. Their story remains a fascinating, if little-known, page in Italian military engineering.

▲ The Caproni CA 2 mounted and secured on a rail transport, leaves the Montecolino base in Iseo destined for the BETASOM submarine base in Bordeaux with the task of attacking New York harbour!

CAPRONI CA-2 CLASS MIDGET SUBMARINE, ITALY 1937-43

▲ CA Class Model 2 midget submarine. This was the model that was later chosen to attempt the epic feat of attacking New York harbour.

CAPRONI CB CLASS

The CB Class: Italy's Daring Adventure in the Black Sea

In the 1930s, Caproni, renowned primarily for its aircraft, ventured into designing Midget submarines. The first "A"-class prototypes, armed with 450 mm torpedoes, proved disappointing: too fragile and unwieldy for offensive missions. However, the experience gained led to an improved version: the CB class, larger, sturdier, and more capable. Thus, the failures of the CA class gave way to the CBs' success. Systematically designed for coastal defense and anti-submarine warfare.

Built by Caproni under engineers Vincenzo Goeta and Franco Spinelli, these 15-meter-long boats were marvels of miniature naval engineering. With a displacement of 36 tons surfaced (45 submerged) and an operational depth of 55 meters, they relied on a 90 HP diesel engine for surface navigation and a 100 HP electric motor for underwater missions. Primary armament consisted of two 450 mm torpedoes, while some units were also fitted with an 8 mm deck machine gun.

In summer 1940, the first two prototypes (CB-1 and CB-2) underwent sea trials, showing remarkable progress. The CBs were far more efficient and stable than their predecessors, though retaining a similar shape. With a crew of 3–4, they could operate with a range of 1,000 nautical miles surfaced and 60 submerged.

From Italy to the Black Sea: Forgotten Feats

Surprisingly, the CBs' baptism of fire occurred not in the *Mare Nostrum* (Mediterranean) but in the Black Sea. After Germany's failure to capture Sevastopol (1941), the Kriegsmarine requested Italian assistance to disrupt Soviet supply lines to Crimea. Thus, in 1942, an Italian flotilla—including six CBs, nine torpedo boats, and five explosive motorboats—was transferred by rail to Yalta under Frigate Captain Francesco Mimbelli, already a hero of the Battle of Crete at Suda Bay.

In just a few months, the small submarines achieved extraordinary results, covering themselves in glory:
- June 15, 1942: CB-3 sank the Soviet submarine SC-213.
- June 17: CB-2 eliminated the submarine S-32 (1,000 tons).

Sevastopol fell in July, but one last success came in August 1943, when CB-4 sank a third submarine, SCH-207.

CA & CB DATA SHEET		
Model-Class	CA	CB
Producer	Officine Caproni di Taliedo e Iseo	
Crew	2	4
Entry and exit from service	1937-1945	1941-1945
Weight (kg)	13.000/16.000	45.000
Engine	Marelli 25 hp electric motor	Diesel 90 hp/ Motor el. 100 hp
Maximum speed	6,25/7 knots (5/6 underwater)	7,5/6,5 knots underwater
Autonomy	700 nautical miles	1000 nautical miles
Users	Ita	Ita-Rom-Deu-URSS-Yug.
Armament	8 charges of 100 kg and 20 bugs	2 x 450mm torpedo launchers
Secondary armament	2 x 450mm torpedo launchers (up to 41)	Two mines
Production	4 pieces	22/26 pieces
Length-Width- Drawing	10,5-1,96-1,83 m	15-3,0-2,5 m

CAPRONI CLASS CA-3 AND 4 MIDGET SUBMARINE, ITALY 1937-43

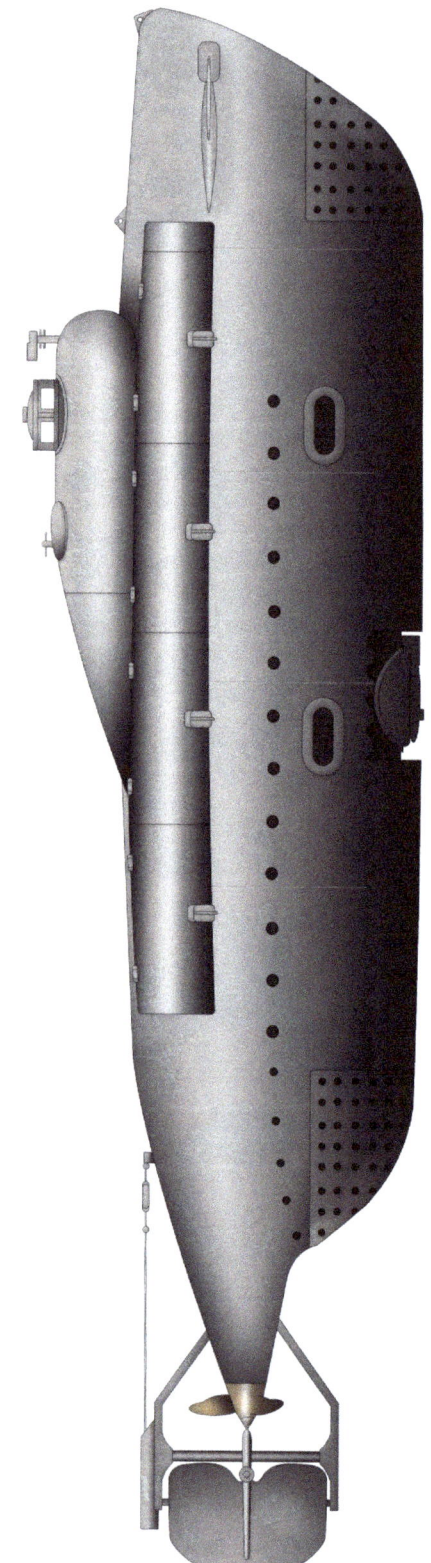

▲ CA Class midget submarine models 3 and 4. This is the latest evolution of the CA class models made in only four pieces.

An Uncertain Fate: From Capture to Oblivion

With the September 8, 1943 armistice, all parameters changed. From allies, Italy became an enemy, and the five surviving CBs in Constanța fell into German hands, later transferred to the Romanian Navy. Others remained with the Italian Social Republic's Navy, which continued the alliance with Germany, though there is no significant evidence of their operational use. The boats in the East were eventually scuttled before the Red Army's arrival in August 1944, while those captured by the Romanians were decommissioned by the Soviets in 1945.

Today, of the 22 completed CBs, only two survive:
- CB-20: Displayed at the Zagreb Museum of Science, recovered after being semi-sunk in Pula in 1945 and later reused by the Yugoslav navy.
- CB-22: Preserved at the Henriquez Museum in Trieste, a silent witness to an era of daring exploits.

The CBs represented a successful weapons system experiment, proving that small, well-engineered units could inflict significant damage. Though their service was brief and localized, their story—of innovation, courage, and oblivion—deserves remembrance as one of the most unusual chapters in Italian naval warfare, like many involving Italy's assault weapons.

Final Notes

The CB-class submarines represented the modern and final evolution of the first Midget submarines deployed during World War I. Specifically designed for coastal defense and anti-submarine warfare, these small but lethal craft were meant to protect Italy's major ports from lurking enemy submarines.

The hull, developed by Major Franco Spinelli of the Naval Engineers, followed the essential lines of the *"Cavallini"* type, characterized by non-pressure-resistant side double bottoms covering about two-thirds of the structure. To simplify production, torpedo tubes were mounted externally to the hull. However, this choice proved problematic: since the tubes weren't watertight, torpedoes were exposed to water for too long, compromising launch reliability during missions.

▲ A CB Class boat of the Italian Navy in the port of Yalta on the Black Sea in 1942. Courtesy photo by Vittorio Vaccà. Author's colouring.

CAPRONI CB CLASS MIDGET SUBMARINE, ITALY 1941-45

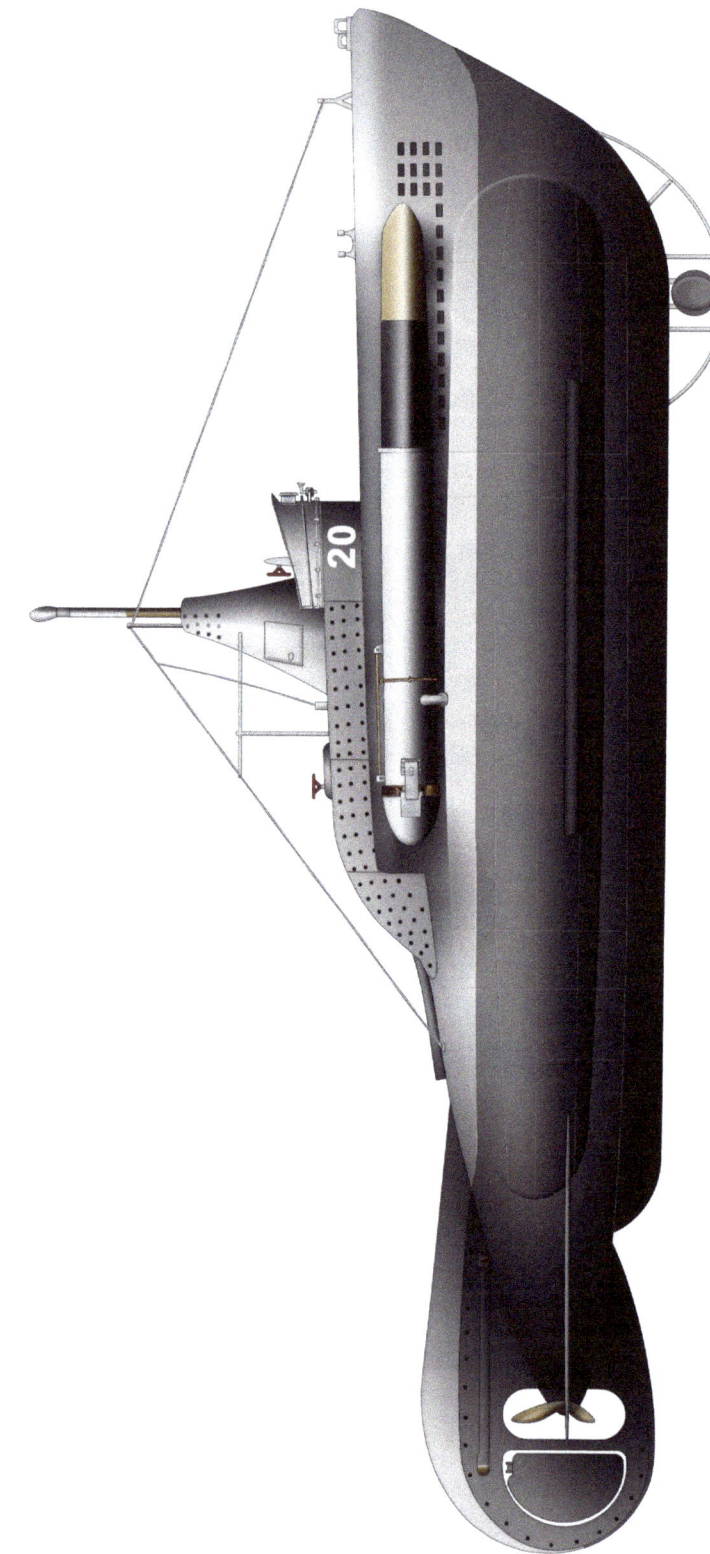

▲ CB-class midget submarine. Compared to the models of the previous class, the CA, these boats were larger. Almost three times as long and with a tonnage of more than 30 tonnealtes more, with an equioage that was twice as high, 4 operators instead of the 2 of the CA class.

Despite their small size and limited displacement, the CBs demonstrated excellent seakeeping, exceeding initial expectations during early trials. Results were so encouraging that, by early 1943, Caproni planned to build 72 units (organized into 12 squadrons of 6 boats each), with a production rate of 6–7 per month. However, events took a different turn. The September 1943 armistice and the need to divert manpower to other wartime priorities led to the project's suspension. By August 1943, 20 of 50 ordered units (40 to Caproni and 10 to AVIS in Castellammare di Stabia) had already been canceled. In the end, only 22 CB-class submarines were completed, of which 12 entered service with the Regia Marina before the armistice. The other 10, still under construction, were finished and used by the Italian Social Republic's Navy.

- Models captured by the Germans after the armistice: 1, 2, 3, 4, 6, 7
- Scuttled: 5
- Units serving with the co-belligerent Southern Army, decommissioned in 1948: 8, 9, 10, 11, 12
- Units serving with the RSI, scuttled, recovered, and decommissioned in 1947: 13, 14, 15, 16, 17, 18, 19, 20, 21, 22, 23, 24, 25, 26

CBs 13, 14, 15, and 16, caught by the armistice in Pula and nearly ready for service, were seized by the Germans and later transferred to the RSI. In fact, on March 22, 1943, 40 units (CB 17/56) had been ordered: 28 were to be built by Caproni in Taliedo and Rovereto, and 12 by AVIS in Castellammare di Stabia, though the latter were never laid down.

The RSI's CBs were primarily used for landing operations and spy recovery behind enemy lines in the Adriatic sector. All were sunk in combat or scuttled by the end of hostilities in May 1945, except CB-19, which returned to the Regia Marina and was dismantled with its counterparts in August 1948.

Materials prepared for subsequent units, from CB-27 onward, were dismantled and recycled postwar.

▲ The decommissioned CB boat in the San Vito depot, in the area of the so-called "Sanza".

CAPRONI CB CLASS CAMOUFLAGE MIDGET SUBMARINE, ITALY 1941-45

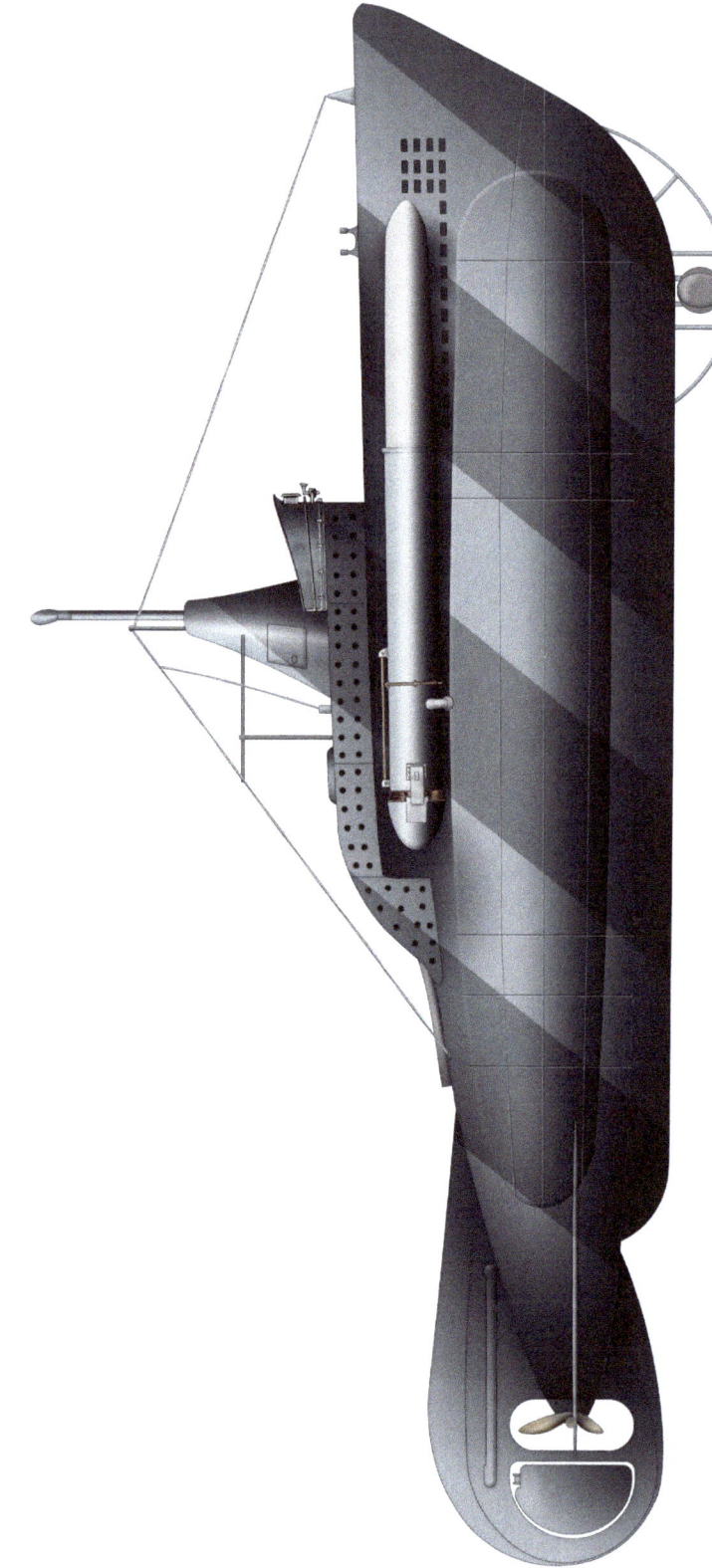

▲ CB-class midget submarine. Compared to the models of the previous class, the CA, these boats were larger. Nearly three times as long and over 30 tons more in tonnage, with a crew that was twice as large, four operators instead of the two of the CA class. This type of camouflage was used by some units in the Black Sea.

▲ A CB Class boat of the Italian Navy in the port of Yalta on the Black Sea in Crimea in 1942. Bundesarchiv.

CAMPINI-BERNARDI MIDGET SUBMARINE, ITALY 1942-1945

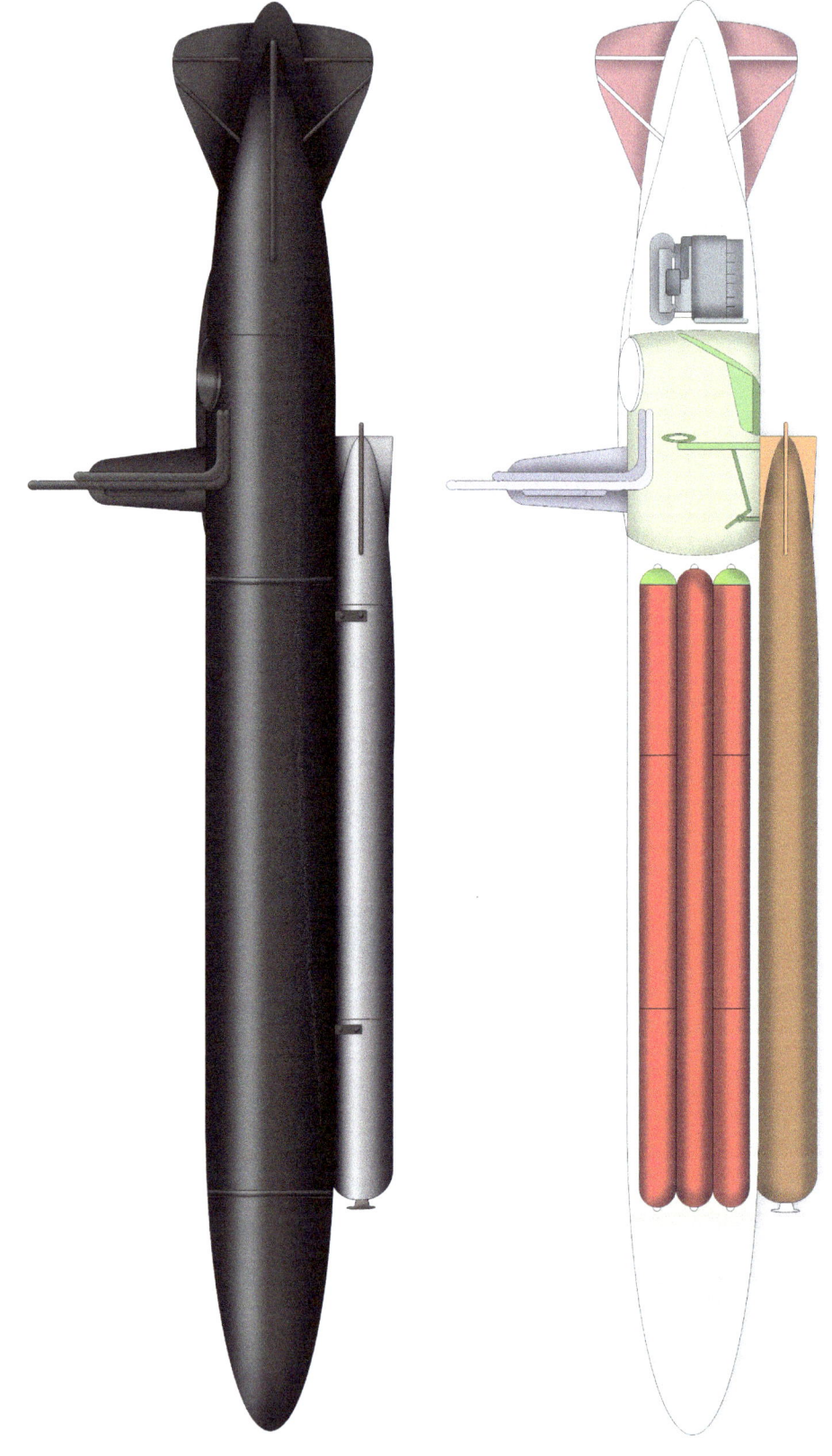

▲ One of the most futuristic machines in the field of advanced mini-submarines was this project by engineer scientist Secondo Campini.

OTHER MIDGET SUBMARINES

■ THE CD CLASS: MINI-SUBMARINES WITH INNOVATIVE PROPULSION

The Italian Navy during World War II developed the CD class, a series of single-seat Midget submarines featuring a water-jet propulsion system for underwater navigation. Designed by engineer Secondo Campini at Caproni's workshops, at least two prototypes were built and tested on Lake Garda.

Origins and Design
In February 1942, the Navy tasked Campini with creating a compact submarine powered by a turbine. The engineer collaborated with Mario De Bernardi, famed test pilot of the Campini-Caproni CC2 jet engine, hence the craft's occasional designation as the Campini-De Bernardi model. The project defined an assault pocket submarine with an oxygen-kerosene turbine for submerged navigation.
Managed by Caproni, with which VENAR (Campini's company founded in 1931 for jet propulsion development) had merged in 1934, the project faced delays due to Allied bombing of Milan in 1943, forcing relocation to Rovereto and later Riva del Garda.
Despite joint interest from the German Kriegsmarine and Imperial Japanese Navy, material shortages and delays prevented prototype completion before the Cassibile Armistice (September 1943). However, the Germans hastily ordered 50 units in March 1944, and at least one or two prototypes were assembled and tested on Lake Garda. The rest were never delivered due to the war's tide turning.

Design and Technology
The single-seat CD submarine had a streamlined, torpedo-like shape to minimize hydrodynamic drag. The pressurized hull housed:
- A periscope with targeting system
- Two 45 cm torpedoes mounted externally beneath the craft
- A retractable conning tower (extending less than a meter when surfaced)

The real innovation lay in the propulsion system: an oxygen-gas turbine ensuring:
- Stealth, avoiding acoustic detection
- No bubbles, reducing detectability
- Greater efficiency than traditional engines

The signed project also included two special variants:

MIDGET SUBMARINE CAMPINI D CLASS DATA SHEET	
Model-Class	Classe D
Producer	Officine Caproni/VENAR di Taliedo e Riva del Garda
Crew	One operator
Entry and exit from service	1942-1945
Weight (kg)	5.500 (5.800 underwater)
Engine	Carraro diesel engine - gas propulsion/turbine engine
Maximum speed	11 knots (30 knots underwater)
Autonomy	240 nautical miles (14 miles underwater)
Interested countries	Italy - Germany - Japan
Armament	2 x 450mm torpedoes
Engine power	60 CV
Production	2 prototypes
Length-Width	11 m - 0,91cm

1. A mine-laying model
2. A net-cutting craft with forward-mounted arms

Fate of the Prototypes

The prototypes' fate remains unclear. Some sources suggest the Germans scuttled them in Garda before retreating, while others indicate the Americans recovered at least one in April 1945, later transporting it to the U.S. for study.

▪ SECONDO CAMPINI: THE ITALIAN PIONEER OF JET PROPULSION

Born in Bologna on August 28, 1904, and passing away in Milan on February 7, 1980, Secondo Campini was one of the most innovative Italian engineers of the twentieth century—a visionary figure and a pioneer in the development of jet propulsion systems for aircraft and naval craft. After graduating in Engineering from the University of Bologna, he moved to Milan in 1931 to bring his jet propulsion theories to life. There, he founded V.E.N.A.R. (*Velivoli E Natanti A Reazione* – Jet Aircraft and Watercraft), through which he developed his first project: a jet-powered motorboat successfully tested in Venice in 1932 on commission from the Ministry of Aeronautics.

Between 1931 and 1934, Campini, well ahead of his time, developed a jet engine for aircraft—the *motoreattore*—a sort of jet airplane that was among the very first in the world. His most famous idea was tied to the Campini-Caproni C.C.2, an experimental aircraft built between 1934 and 1940, capable of reaching 500 km/h at an altitude of 3,000 meters. In 1941, it completed a demonstration flight from Milan to Guidonia, but the project was not pursued further due to wartime priorities. Another notable creation was the submarine described earlier in this text.

Campini also devised numerous futuristic projects that remained on paper only: stratospheric monoplanes, jet fighters and bombers, and a twin-engine bomber (1942–43). After 1945, Campini was recruited in the United States, where he also worked on military projects such as the YB-35. His career was crowned by the Marconi Foundation Award, bestowed on him by the Emilian Group of the Knights of Labor for his contributions to aeronautical engineering. A frequently forgotten pioneer, his story is that of a brilliant mind whose ideas surpassed the limits of his time, earning him a place among the greats of global engineering.

▲ Campini surrounded by workers next to his best-known project, the C.C.2 fighter jet.

THE S.A. 1-2-3 ASSAULT SUBMARINES – THE MYSTERIES OF BAIA

The Minisini-Ferretti Project: a technological vanguard in the history of midget submarines

Between late 1939 and early 1940, an ambitious project began to take shape—one that would leave its mark on the history of military underwater craft: the Minisini-Ferretti midget submarine, also known as the S.A. (d'assalto – assault) submarines. These boats were even more widely known—though shrouded in mystery—by their exotic nicknames: Sandokan, Yanez, and Kammamurì. The project was completed within the same year and represented a bold attempt to combine compactness, power, and advanced technology at a time when the naval arms race was driving increasingly experimental solutions.

This vessel was conceived by General of Naval Weapons Eugenio Minisini, then Director of the Torpedo Factory in Baia (Pozzuoli). Minisini was no stranger to innovations that would revolutionize naval warfare: he was already famous for designing the "side-impulse torpedo launcher", a mechanism adopted on all Italian MAS torpedo boats by the late 1930s. This innovation remained in service even after the war, equipping Italy's torpedo boats for decades.

A revolutionary submarine

The S.A. assault submarine stood out for its compact size and displacement of just 13 tons. It was powered by a 350-hp Isotta-Fraschini thermal engine, with a unique feature: its fuel system had been modified to run on an alcohol-oxygen mixture, an experimental solution developed as early as 1936 by Professor Ferretti.

This configuration, at least in theory, promised even greater power potential but above all represented a historical turning point: it was the first closed-cycle thermal engine to successfully pass all bench tests. A remarkable milestone, considering that at the time, similar international attempts had failed due to the technological limitations of the era. Only

▲ The base-silurificio di Baia (Pozzuoli) where the S.A. vehicles were built. In the small photo: the islet of San Patrizio connected to the base by a jetty, the true Santa Santorum of the project.

ITALIAN NAVY SPECIAL FORCES WWII

MIDGET ASSAULT SUBMARINE S.A "SANDOKAN", ITALY 1941-1945

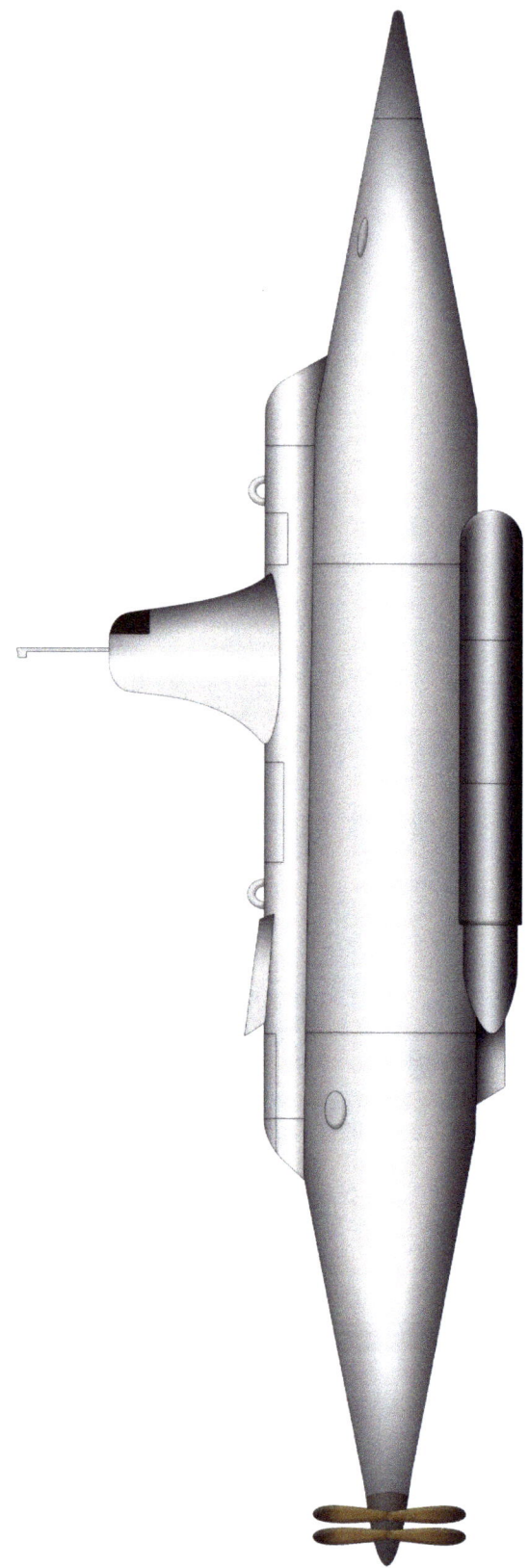

▲ A truly mysterious story surrounds these special Navy vehicles classified as S.A.

recently—excluding nuclear propulsion—has this technology found real-world application in advanced projects like the U 212A class submarines, now in service with the Italian Navy.

Prototypes and their features
A first series of two or three prototypes was developed:
- SA 1, completed in 1941 – nicknamed *Sandokan*
- SA 2, finished the following year – nicknamed *Yanez*

These vessels could reach a speed of 15 knots, sustainable for up to two hours. Externally, they featured a truly unusual configuration, with two coaxial counter-rotating tractor propellers located at the bow. Armament consisted of two 450 mm torpedoes mounted at the stern.

The operational concept envisioned the vessel being transported by a destroyer or specially equipped boat and released near the target. Once submerged, it would attack enemy formations at high speed, following a direct route.

Evolution: SA 3 and the fate of the prototypes
Tests conducted on the two prototypes in 1942 revealed some issues, leading to the development of a third prototype, the SA 3, which incorporated significant improvements. The new version featured a more conventional and advanced design, along with a more powerful engine, again designed by Engineer Ferretti, capable of propelling the submarine to over 20 knots underwater.

However, the collapse of Fascist Italy marked the end of the project. By September 8, 1943, the SA 1 and SA 2 were already decommissioned at the torpedo factory and were dismantled—although some components were recovered by the Americans and transferred to the USA along with Minisini. This led to a joint Italo-American program for a new 30-ton midget submarine, but the initiative was abandoned in 1957 due to technical problems and high costs.

Although these assault submarines never saw large-scale combat use, their development was a pioneering experiment, anticipating solutions that would only become reality decades later. Even today, years later, their contribution to military underwater technology remains an example of ingenuity and technological courage.

▲ The captions accompanying this photo describe the vehicle as S.A.3 Kammamurì as it leaves the Baia factory after its completion. Author's colouring.

▲▼ Series of shots taken by the US Army relating to the dismantling of the two boats SA 1 and 2 in the area of the torpedo factory in Baia (Pozzuioli). Author's colouring. US Archives in PD.

The surprising thing is also the fact that, certainly due to the secrecy of the entire programme and the subsequent events surrounding the armistice of 8 September 1943, there is no trace of documentation or anything else about these projects in the archives of the Naval Historical Office. Apart from direct evidence of this history, there is nothing tangible or written.

In contrast, at the US archives dependent on the US Library of Congress in Washington, there is a wealth of Italian naval technical documentation dating back to the Second World War. These include several of the images showing the collection and transport to the USA of the SA1 and SA2 prototypes from the Baia torpedo factory.

All this happened even though today we know how things actually went: the overall project "was" immediately authorised by the General Staff of the Navy under the old original acronym SA (Sommergibile d'Assalto - Assault Submarine) given in 1936, and was covered as already mentioned by the utmost secrecy. Once the design was completed, the small submarine was laid down at the Baia factory in 1941 and was completed at the beginning of the following year. The Navy's interest in the new unit and the pressure from the Head of the Government "were such" that the General Staff authorised, a couple of months after the first boat was laid down, a second unit, also assigned to the same torpedo factory and destined to optimise the test periods.

To the torpedo boat, the workers and the managers of the factory themselves, with the help of a highly successful adventure film being shown at that time in Italian cinemas based on Salgari's novels, assigned the nickname of *Sandokan*, and to its twin that of *Yanez*.

■ FURTHER ON THE S.A. 3 PROTOTYPE - KAMMAMURÌ

The mystery of the SA 3: the advanced-design submarine lost in the chaos of the Armistice.

It is now well established that the SA 3 prototype, the last of the three submarines built at Baia, represented a significant qualitative leap compared to its predecessors, SA 1 and SA 2. With a submerged speed exceeding 20 knots, as confirmed by experimental trials, this vessel introduced major structural modifications, including a "beaver-tail" shaped stern, with integrated depth rudders and a pair of elevated directional rudders. Its armament consisted of two 450 mm torpedo tubes, installed in the non-pressure hull and aimed toward the stern.

Stability while submerged was ensured by a Riva Calzoni hydraulic servomotor, connected to a hydrostatic system similar to those used in torpedoes. However, the development of the SA 3 was hindered by extreme secrecy (despite the well-known fact that the Baia torpedo factory was a sieve in terms of security...), repeated redesigns, and—by spring 1943—the worsening of the war situation.

S.A. 1-2-3 DATA SHEET		
Model-Class	S.A 1 e 2	S.aA. 3
Producer	Silurificio di Baia (Pozzuoli)	
Crew	3	4
Entry and exit from service	1937-1943	1941-1945
Weight (kg)	13.000	13.000
Engine	Isotta Fraschini 350 hp	Closed-cycle diesel 40 hp
Maximum speed	13,5 knots (15 underwater)	15 knots/20 underwater
Autonomy	100 nautical miles	1000 nautical miles
Users	Italy	Italy
Armament	2 x 450mm torpedo launchers	2/3 x 450mm torpedo launchers
Autonomy underwater	2 hours	2 hours
Production	2 prototypes	1 prototype
Length-Width	13-1,5 m	13-1,5 m

Although Engineer Ferretti had theorized the possibility of reaching 25 knots using an exothermic turbine engine, the fate of the submarine, for all these reasons, remains shrouded in mystery.

One of the unresolved enigmas of the Mediterranean war involves a mysterious incident that occurred to a U.S. cruiser off the coast of Salerno on the night between September 8 and 9, 1943. While the episode has been officially attributed to German guided bombs, torpedo bombers, or the submarine *Vellela*, an alternative theory suggests that the real culprit may have been the SA 3 Kammamurì.

Indeed, the submarine—not yet officially delivered to the Royal Italian Navy, but undergoing operational trials with a military crew—departed from Baia on the afternoon of September 8 for a final test mission and never returned. At 7:30 p.m., carefully camouflaged with netting, it left the torpedo factory aboard its support vessel, unaware that the Armistice had been proclaimed just a few hours earlier.

It is a fact that, thanks in part to complex espionage maneuvers involving both U.S. forces and the Mafia, the Americans managed to lay their hands on the project's documents. At the time, the SA 3 represented a masterpiece of underwater engineering: the first submarine in the world with stealth navigation and unlimited range, equipped with a closed-cycle engine that would only be replicated much later by the most modern U-boats. Today, only rare period photographs taken by personnel at the Baia shipyard remain. But the mystery endures. What happened to the Kammamuri? Does it lie in some secret hangar of the Italian Navy, dismantled and forgotten? Some have claimed that its revolutionary engine was seen in a nautical factory in Zingonia (Bergamo). Or, following the supposed attack and damage to the American cruiser, did it sink with its crew, and now the wreck lies at the bottom of Pozzuoli Bay?

More than eighty years after its disappearance, the SA 3 remains one of the great unsolved mysteries of naval history—a symbol of technological excellence erased by war and oblivion.

▲ Another photograph taken by the US Army relating to the dismantling of the two boats SA 1 and 2 in the area of the torpedo factory in Baia (Pozzuioli). Author's colouring. US Arches in PD.

CLASS CM & CC SUBMARINES

■ THE CM CLASS: THE REGIA MARINA'S LIGHT SUBMARINES

Within the military and strategic context of 1930s Italy, the Regia Marina entrusted the Cantieri Riuniti dell'Adriatico (CRDA) in Monfalcone with the task of developing a new type of underwater craft: compact, quick to build, and suitable for mass operations against enemy units transiting through chokepoints such as the Sicilian Channel. The project took shape in 1937, but only in April 1943, on the eve of Italy's military collapse, was it updated and definitively approved, assuming the designation "CM," an acronym for either *Costiero Monfalcone* or *Costiero Modificato* (Coastal Monfalcone/Modified Coastal). These were true midget submarines, based on a simple-hull structure with internal double bottoms. The core idea was clear: to provide the Italian Navy with low-cost, mass-producible units, suitable for both coastal defense and targeted offensive missions.

Technical characteristics

CM-class submarines measured 32.9 meters in length and 2.89 meters in beam, with a draft of 2.77 meters. Displacement ranged from 92 tons surfaced to 114 tons submerged, and maximum operational depth reached 80 meters. The crew was kept to a minimum: two officers and four petty officers or sailors. For surface propulsion, the CM class was equipped with two diesel engines totaling 660 hp, derived from those used on the P26/40 tank, which had just entered production at the time. Underwater propulsion was provided by two 120-hp electric motors. Performance was modest but adequate for their role: 14 knots on the surface, 6 knots submerged, with a range of 2,000 nautical miles at 9 knots surfaced and approximately 70 nautical miles at 4 knots underwater. Armament consisted of two fixed 450 mm torpedo tubes mounted at the bow, with no reloading capability. An anti-aircraft twin 13.2 mm machine gun on a retractable mount was originally planned but never installed.

Construction and fate

The order for the first prototype, named CM 1, was followed in May 1943 by plans for two additional units (CM 2 and CM 3), with the intention of eventually building nineteen submarines. At the same time, an identical model was commissioned from Caproni, which modified it to create the distinct "CC" class (see next chapter).
Construction took place at the CRDA shipyards in Monfalcone. However, events moved quickly: the Armistice of September 8, 1943, plunged Italy into chaos. Only CM 1 was launched before the armistice. It was captured by the Germans a few days later and initially incorporated into the Kriegsmarine as U.IT 17, before being handed over to the Repubblican National Navy.

▲ The submarine CM 1 returning to base after some trials at the end of 1944. Courtesy Edizioni Albertelli.

CM AND CC CLASS LIGHT SUBMARINES, ITALY 1941-1945

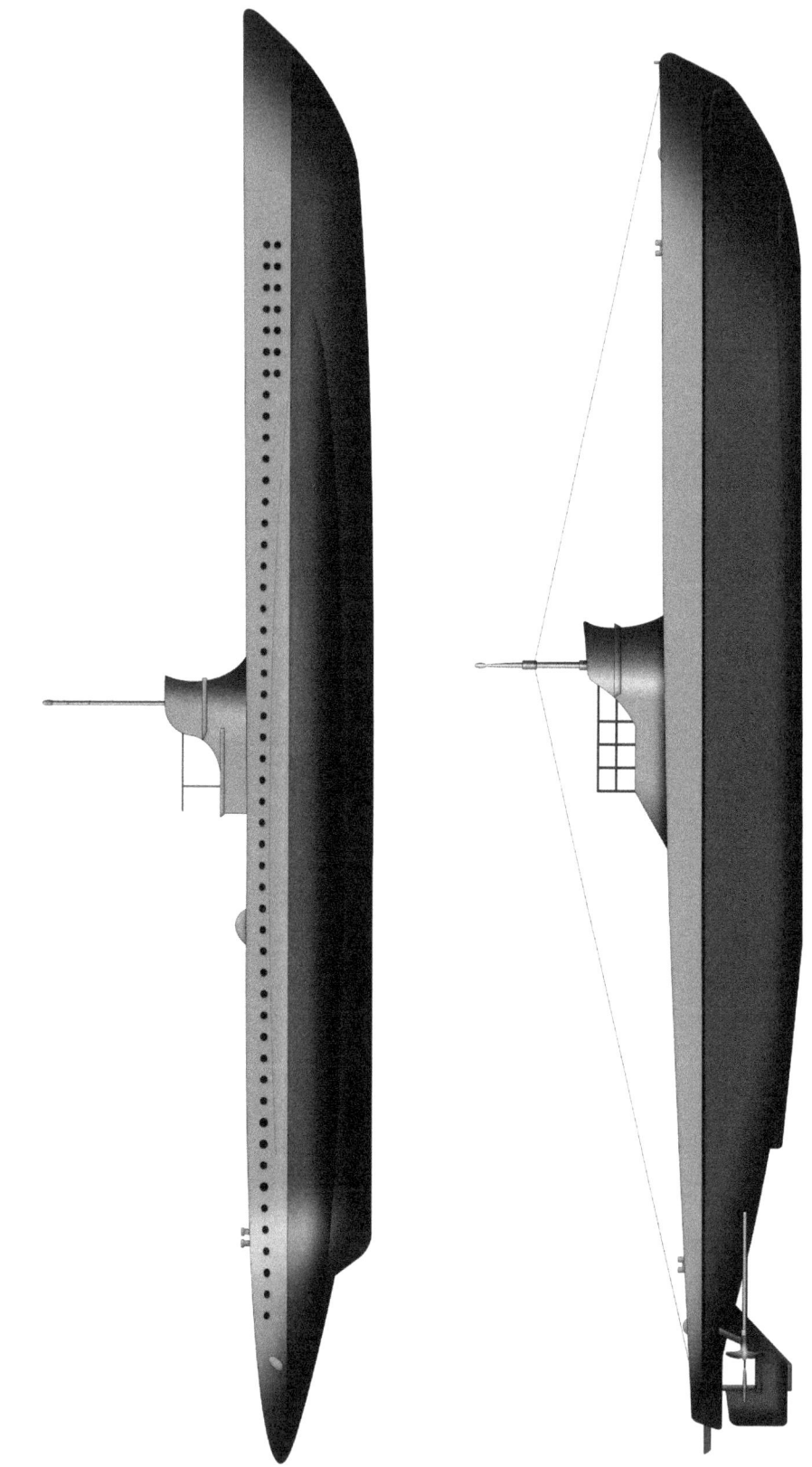

◂ A truly mysterious story surrounds these special Navy vehicles classified as S.A.

Completed in December 1944, it was officially commissioned on January 5, 1945, in Pola, but it never saw active service. On April 29, 1945, it surrendered to Allied forces in Venice, was later returned to the Regia Marina, and decommissioned in 1948.

CM 2, still under construction at the time of the Armistice, was also captured by the Germans and provisionally assigned to the Kriegsmarine (as U.IT 18), then handed over to the Repubblican Navy. Launched in February 1944, it was damaged by a bombing raid and abandoned unfinished. The hull was later cut and displayed at the Henriquez Museum in Trieste for about fifteen years before being permanently scrapped. The third unit, CM 3, was never completed and was dismantled directly on the slipway.

Assessment and conclusion

Although they never took part in wartime operations, the CM-class submarines represent an interesting example of the Regia Marina's desire to adopt rapid and flexible solutions in response to an increasingly critical military situation. More advanced than the earlier CB-class submarines, yet limited by their small size and historical circumstances, the CM class remains today a little-known but significant chapter in Italian naval engineering during World War II.

▲ The CM submarine as it is about to be launched. Courtesy Edizioni Albertelli.

Class CC & CM DATA SHEET		
Model-Class	CM	CC
Producer	CRDA	Caproni Taliedo
Crew	8	8
Entry and exit from service	1943-1945	1943-1945
Weight	92 t/114 t underwater	117 t
Engine	Disel Fiat-SPA 660 CV	Diesel Fiat da 700 hp
Maximum speed	14 knots (6 underwater)	14 knots/9 underwater
Autonomy	2000 nautical miles	1200 nautical miles
Users	Italy	Italy
Armament	2 x 450mm torpedo launchers	3 x 450mm torpedo launchers
Secondary armament	2 x 13.2 mm machine guns	Breda M.31 binary machine gun
Production	3 units	3 units
Length-Widt	33 -2,9 m	33 -2,9 m

THE CC CLASS: THE CAPRONI LIGHT SUBMARINES

Designed as an evolution of the earlier CM class, the CC-class midget submarines (*Costiero Caproni* – Coastal Caproni) represented an attempt by the Regia Marina to strengthen its submarine fleet during the final years of World War II. Commissioned in 1943 from the Caproni company of Taliedo, these submarines were intended to form a fast and modern coastal strike force. However, of the 37 units initially planned, only three were started, and none were completed due to the events that followed the Italian Armistice.

The CC-class submarines were a revised version of the earlier CM-class, differing primarily in stern design and slightly improved performance. Measuring 33 meters in length (compared to 32.5 for the CM), with a surface displacement of 99.5 tons and 117 tons submerged, and a maximum operating depth of 80 meters, these submarines were conceived for fast, offensive missions.

Their propulsion system included two 700-hp Fiat diesel engines for surface navigation and two 120-hp CRDA electric motors for underwater movement, providing a top speed of 14 knots surfaced and 9 knots submerged. Their operational range reached 1,200 miles at 10 knots on the surface and 70 miles at 4 knots underwater, making them well-suited for coastal operations.

Armament and Crew: Small but Deadly

The offensive armament was centered around three 450 mm torpedo tubes (one more than the CM class), each with a single spare torpedo. Air defense was provided by a twin-mounted 13.2 mm Breda Mod. 31 machine gun. The crew, kept to a minimum, consisted of two officers and six petty officers or sailors—a typical configuration for midget submarines of the time.

On June 19, 1943, the Regia Marina, recognizing the improvements introduced by Caproni, officially placed an order for three units (CC 1, CC 2, and CC 3), with plans to produce an additional 34 submarines thereafter. However, on September 8, 1943, following the proclamation of the Armistice and the German occupation, all work was suspended. It briefly resumed under the Repubblican Navy, but the project was definitively canceled in December 1944, when the three units were less than 50% complete.

▲ Interesting picture showing two classes of Italian mini-submarines from World War II. In the foreground two pieces of the CB class, and in the background the CM 1 at Monfalcone. Courtesy Edizioni Albertelli.

SPECIAL TRANSPORT SUBMARINES

▪ SLC TRANSPORT SUBMARINES – THE CASE OF SCIRÈ

The story of the Scirè, a submarine of the Regia Marina, is legendary. It became famous for transporting slow-running torpedoes (SLCs) used in the Alexandria raid and other missions with the Italian Navy's assault units. Like others in its squadron, the submarine was named after a region in Ethiopia—*Scirè* in this case. Its chronicle illustrates the level of success achieved by the Navy's special operations units.

The Transformation of the Scirè and Its First Missions
The Scirè was assigned to the X^a MAS Flotilla and converted into a *delivery platform* for SLCs (Siluri a Lenta Corsa). Between August and September 1940, several modifications were made:
- Removal of the 100/47 Mod. 1935 deck gun, two torpedoes, and other nonessential materials
- Reduction of the conning tower's size
- Installation of three watertight cylinders (two aft and one forward) for SLC transport, capable of withstanding depths of up to 90 meters

To improve camouflage, the Scirè was repainted in light green, a tone chosen to blend in with the night sky. Additionally, the silhouette of a fishing boat was painted on the hull to deceive the enemy. Command was entrusted to Lieutenant Commander Junio Valerio Borghese.

The Gibraltar Missions
- Operation B.G. 1 (September 1940) – On September 24, the *Scirè* departed La Spezia to attack the British base at Gibraltar. However, on September 29, due to the departure of Force H, the mission was canceled and the submarine returned.
- Operation B.G. 2 (October 1940) – On October 21, the *Scirè* left again carrying three SLCs and six operators: Tesei, Pedretti, Birindelli, Paccagnini, Durand de la Penne, and Bianchi. Despite difficulties crossing the Strait of Gibraltar, the SLCs were released on October 30. Unfortunately, all three experienced technical issues. Though unsuccessful, the mission provided valuable lessons for future operations.
- Operation B.G. 3 (May 1941) – On May 15, the *Scirè* set off again for Gibraltar, but once more, the SLCs failed, and the mission was aborted.
- Operation B.G. 4 (September 1941) – On September 10, the *Scirè* sailed again. This time, the SLCs succeeded in damaging three ships: *Durham* (auxiliary cruiser), *Fiona Shell* (tanker) and *HMS Denbydale* (tanker).

The Alexandria Raid (December 1941)
The most famous mission was Operation G.A. 3, targeting the British naval base at Alexandria, Egypt.
- Departure: December 3 from La Spezia
- Targets successfully hit or damaged: HMS Valiant (battleship) – severely damaged, HMS Queen Elizabeth (flagship) – knocked out of service for 18 months, Sagona (tanker) and HMS Jervis (destroyer) – damaged

All operators were captured but later awarded the Gold Medal of Military Valor. The Scirè itself also received the highest military honors.

The Final Mission and Sinking (1942)
In the summer of 1942, under the command of Lieutenant Bruno Zelik, the Scirè was sent on a mission to Haifa carrying 11 Gamma men (underwater commandos).
- Departure: July 27, 1942, from La Spezia
- Arrival at Leros: August 2

However, on August 10, 1942, while approaching Haifa harbor, the Scirè was detected and sunk by British forces, with the loss of the entire crew.

SCIRÈ SUBMARINE IN SLC CARRIER VERSION, ITALY 1937-1942

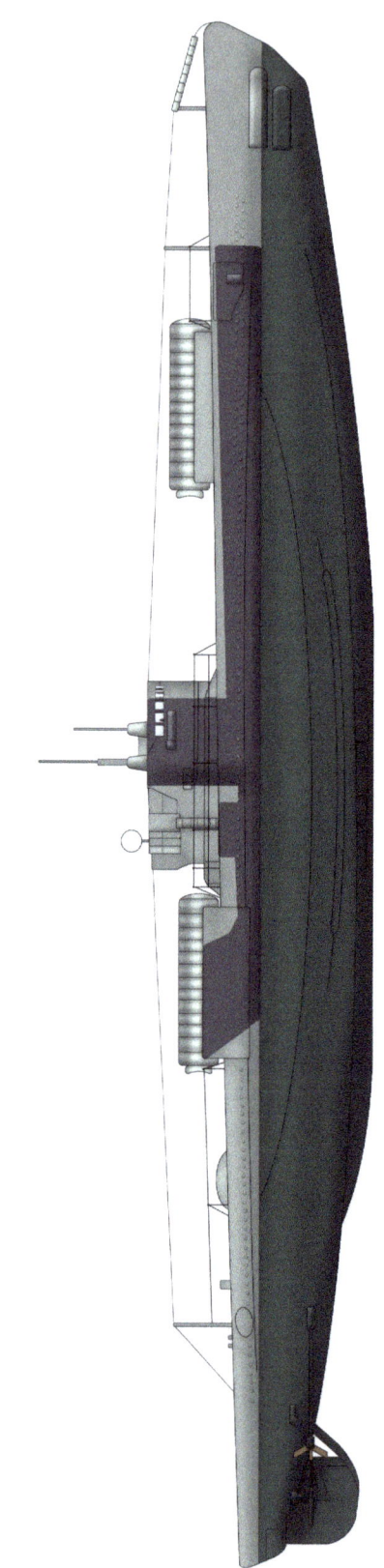
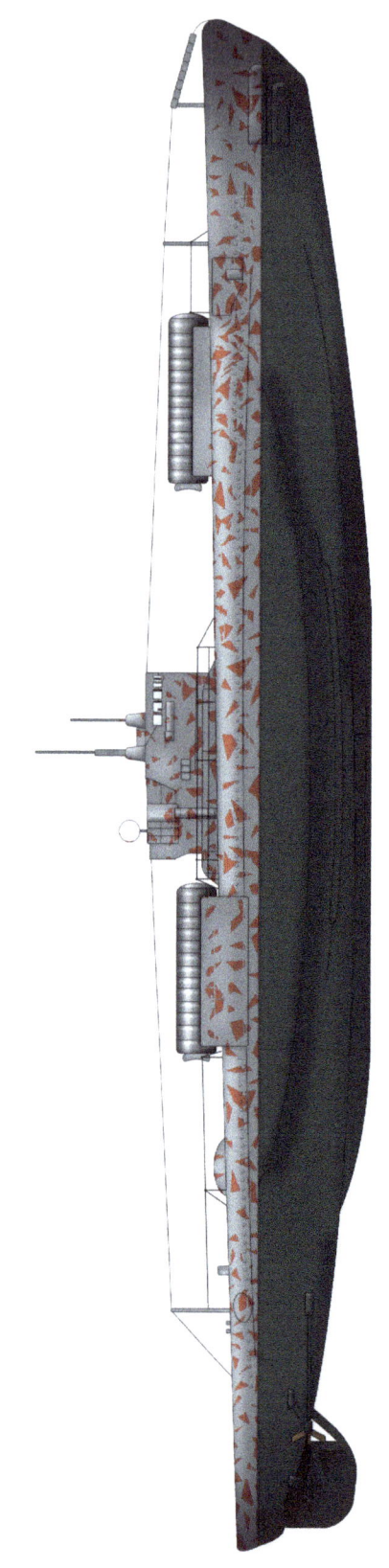

▲ The submarine Sciré, shown here in two different camouflages, was completed at the end of April 1939. Later, together with other boats, it was converted to carry "Slow Running Torpedoes" (SLC), more commonly known as "Pigs". The Sciré displaced 856 t in immersion. (683 when surfacing), was 60 m long overall.

Conclusion

The Scirè and the Xᵃ MAS Flotilla wrote heroic pages in Italian naval history, demonstrating bravery, ingenuity, and determination in extremely high-risk missions. Their exploits remain, to this day, examples of daring and military skill.

▲ One of the SLC container cylinders recovered from the wreck of the Scirè off the coast of Haifa in Israel is now at the Naval Technical Museum in La Spezia.

▼ Two open SLC containers mounted on a submersible conveyor.

▲ The submarine *Gondar*, another SLC carrier, with the four assault craft containers, the famous pigs. On the later submarines Scirè and Ambra, equipped to force enemy ships, the containers were reduced to three, one at the bow and two at the stern of the turret.

▲ The submarine *Scirè* (with three SLC assault craft canisters on deck), one at the bow and two at the stern, sailing in the La Spezia harbour. It was commanded by Lieutenant Commander Prince Junio Valerio Borghese.

CA TRANSPORT SUBMARINES – THE LEONARDO DA VINCI

The Leonardo da Vinci, a submarine of the Regia Marina, distinguished itself as the most effective Italian submarine of World War II, and the most successful non-German submarine overall. With 17 ships sunk, totaling 120,243 gross register tons, its record remains unsurpassed in the history of the Italian Navy.

Operational History
- 1940: First missions in the Atlantic

After a training period with the 22nd Squadron in Naples, the *Da Vinci* was sent to the Atlantic. On September 22, 1940, under the command of Lieutenant Commander Ferdinando Calda, it crossed the Strait of Gibraltar, narrowly escaping an intense anti-submarine attack. In the following days, it attempted—unsuccessfully—to hit the auxiliary cruiser *Cilicia* and an armed transport, enduring a counterattack from the British aircraft carrier *Argus*. Despite difficulties, it reached BETASOM in Bordeaux, the Italian base in the Atlantic, on October 31.

- 1941: Between success and setbacks: December 1940 – January 1941: On a mission west of Ireland, it failed to sink the steamer *Bodnant* and survived a depth charge attack; April 1941: An unsuccessful patrol off the Irish coast; June 1941: First major success – the sinking of the tanker *Auris* (8,030 tons); September–October 1941: New missions with sightings but few results, until command was passed to Commander Luigi Longanesi Cattani.
- 1942: The year of triumphs. Under the command of Lieutenant Gianfranco Gazzana-Priaroggia, the *Da Vinci* became a true scourge for the Allies: February: Sank the Brazilian steamer *Cabedelo* and the Latvian ship *Everasma*; June: Sunk the schooner *Reine Marie Stuart*, the motor ship *Chile*, and two other merchant ships; November–December: A series of sinkings including the steamer *Andreas*, the motor ship *Marcus Whitman*, and the freighter *Veerhaven*.
- 1943: The final and boldest mission. Refitted for special operations, the *Da Vinci* ventured into the Indian Ocean, achieving its greatest victory: March 14: Sank the British liner *Empress of Canada (21,517 tons), the largest ship ever sunk by an Italian submarine; April: An extraordinary series of sinkings, including the steamer *Sembilan*, the motor ship *Manaar*, and the tanker *Doryssa*.

▲The oceanic submarine Leonardo da Vinci returning from a victorious mission to the Betasom base in Bordeaux and being received with military honours. The Leonardo da Vinci was the number one ace of all Italian submarines during the World War.

ITALIAN NAVY SPECIAL FORCES WWII

OCEANIC SUBMARINE LEONARDO DA VINCI, ITALY 1938-1942

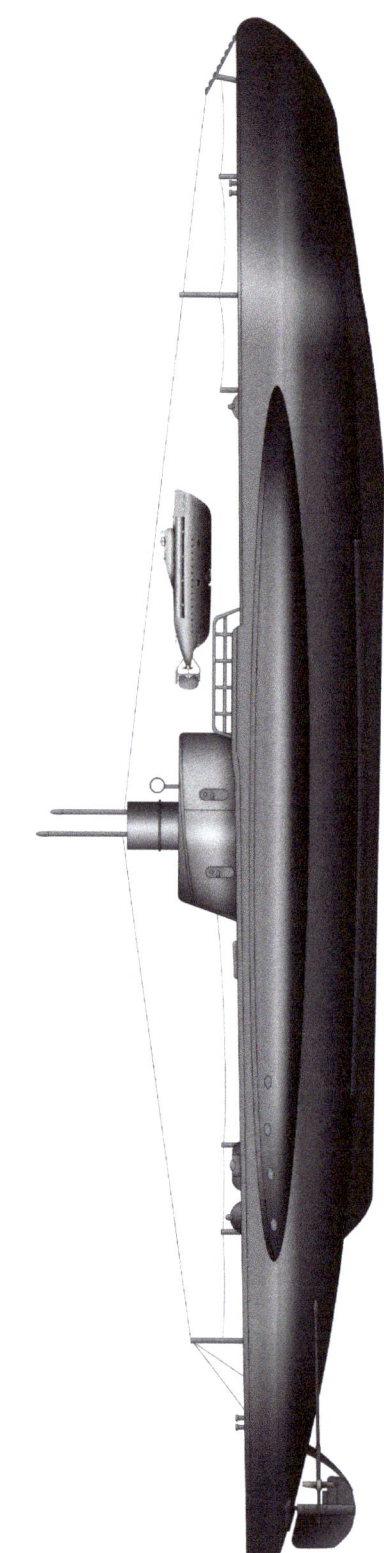

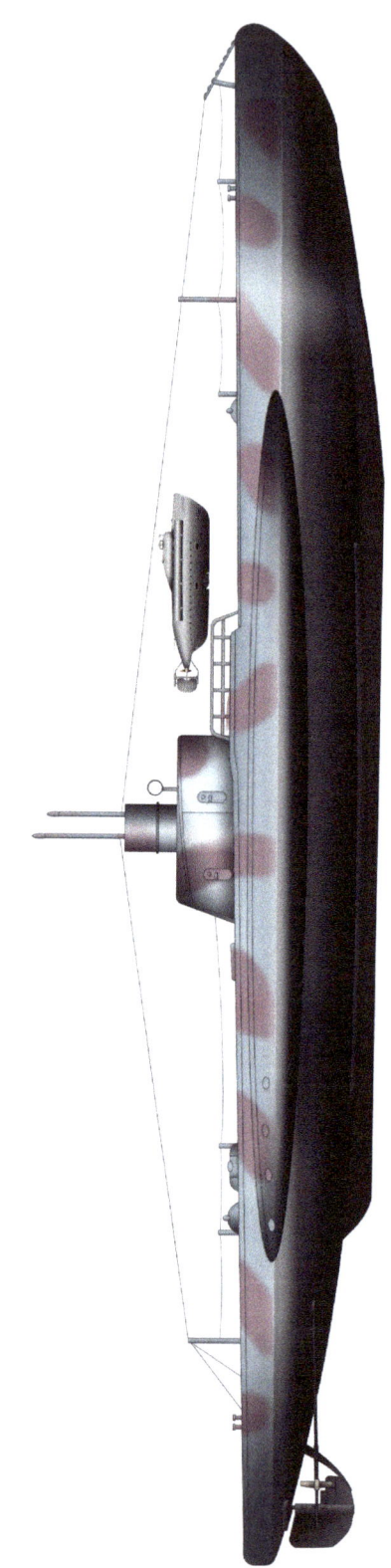

▲ The Marconi-class ocean-going submarine Leonardo da Vinci was tasked in 1943 to attempt the famous "attack on New York," carrying on its bridge a miniature CA submarine prepared for just such an attack.

Heroic End: "It sank with honor, fighting to the last torpedo"

On May 23, 1943, while returning to Europe, the Da Vinci was detected and attacked by British destroyers off Vigo. After a violent depth charge bombardment, the submarine disappeared beneath the sea, taking with it the entire crew, including Commander Gazzana-Priaroggia, who was posthumously awarded the Gold Medal of Military Valor.

In 12 war missions, the submarine covered 66,637 nautical miles on the surface and 3,261 submerged, demonstrating exceptional daring and technical skill. Even today, its name symbolizes Italian naval excellence during World War II.

THE DARING PLAN TO ATTACK NEW YORK

In the summer of 1942, Prince Junio Valerio Borghese, commander of the Xª MAS Flotilla, conceived an unprecedented operation: an attack on the port of New York, the very symbol of American economic and military power. The goal was to deliver a devastating psychological blow, proving that even U.S. shores were not safe. For this mission, the submarine *Leonardo da Vinci* was chosen as the delivery vessel. The choice was no coincidence: the *Da Vinci* was one of the most reliable submarines at BETASOM, and its long-range capability made it ideal for such a risky and extended mission.

The CA Class: A Secret Weapon Transported by Train

The key element of the operation was the CA-class midget submarine, an assault craft designed for stealth missions. For the occasion, the small submarine was secretly transported by train from northern Italy to Bordeaux. The CA 2 would then be mounted onto the *Da Vinci*, housed in a recess created by removing the bow gun.

The complex operation was to be led by Lieutenant Eugenio Massano, personally dispatched by Borghese. Onboard the CA with him would be two Gamma men—the legendary assault divers of the Xª MAS—armed with 28 explosive charges ranging from 20 to 100 kg each. The audacious plan was to infiltrate New York Harbor, mine anchored ships, and unleash chaos before disappearing into the Hudson River.

Technical Trials: Underwater Release

Between August and September 1942, the *Da Vinci* underwent structural modifications to accommodate the CA 2, while intensive training began simultaneously. The most critical tests involved the release and recovery of the midget submarine while submerged at a depth of 12 meters.

Under the expert guidance of Massano, who had trained extensively at the secret base in Montecolino on Lake Iseo, the trials yielded promising results: the CA 2 could be released and, in theory, recovered. However, the designers knew that recovery would be nearly impossible under real-world conditions. As a backup plan, it was intended that, after the attack, the Gamma men would scuttle the CA and reach land in disguise, perhaps attempting to escape through Manhattan itself.

The End of the Dream: Sinking of the Da Vinci and the Armistice

Sadly, fate intervened. On May 23, 1943, during its return from the Indian Ocean, the *Leonardo da Vinci* was detected and sunk by British units off Vigo, along with its commander, Gazzana-Priaroggia, already a hero of multiple exploits.

With the submarine's loss, the New York mission was postponed and ultimately canceled following the Italian Armistice on September 8, 1943. Had it gone ahead, it would have been the first enemy attack on American soil since 1812—a dramatic act that could have reshaped American perceptions of the war.

The New York attack plan remains one of the boldest missions ever conceived by the Italian Navy, a mix of courage, technology, and operational imagination that anticipated the tactics of modern commandos. Had it been executed, it might have written an entirely different chapter in the naval history of World War II—a plan worthy of an Ian Fleming novel, lost to the tides of history at the last moment.

▲ The Leonardo da Vinci in three period pictures, in the one below you can see very clearly the special nest built in the space intended for the submarine's forward gun. Inside it, the Caproni CA 2 mini-submarine that was to attempt the epic feat has already been placed.

THE SECRET BASES OF THE ASSAULT UNITS

■ MONTECOLINO, THE GARDA TUNNEL, AND BAIA (POZZUOLI)

Equally important were the sites where these special weapons were conceived, built, and assembled. A sort of Italian Peenemünde—though the comparison may be a bit exaggerated. Nonetheless, these secret facilities were where Italy's naval secret weapons were born. In addition to the torpedo factory at Baia near Pozzuoli and the military perimeter around La Spezia—which were not truly secret given their known role as arsenals and military workshops—here we focus on two truly clandestine bases, both involved in the development of lethal underwater weapons.
We're talking about the Montecolino base, near Iseo on the lake of the same name, and the base located in the so-called Adige–Garda Tunnel, whose entrance is in Mori and outlet in the municipality of Nago-Torbole, both in Trentino.

■ MONTECOLINO: THE CAPRONI BASE FOR SEAPLANES AND MIDGET SUBMARINES

The Secrets of Montecolino: The Ghost Operation to Strike the Heart of New York
Amid the calm waters of Lake Iseo, hidden among the vegetation of the Montecolino peninsula, lies a story worthy of a war thriller. What now appears to be a forgotten ruin was once the site of top-secret projects designed to strike the enemy where he least expected it: the port of New York.
In the early 20th century, Montecolino was considered the ideal location for a seaplane training school, protected from the lake's winds. After World War I, the area went quiet until 1930, when Caproni set up an experimental outpost for its seaplanes.
A kind of hidden base. But with the outbreak of World War II, this abandoned factory became the nerve center of a bold, nearly impossible mission: a direct attack on the United States. The plan involved the development of midget submarines—secret weapons for impossible missions. Although the Regia Mari-

▲ Current aerial view (Google Maps) of the entire area occupied at the time by the Caproni base on the Montecolino peninsula in the municipality of Provaglio Iseo, a few kilometres from Iseo on the lake of the same name.

▲▼ Series of images of the Montecolino base, from the period and today, taken by the author. Above: the row of sheds for the manufacture of seaplanes and mini-submarines. Below from left: the testing workshop building, followed by the now decaying interior of the sheds. Note the inscription in German: Rauchen Verboten (No Smoking).

na had performed well in conventional clashes with the British fleet, it had also fostered an unexpected weapon that had proven devastating in combat: the raiders of the X^a MAS Flotilla. Fearless men, capable of astounding feats such as the sinking of the battleships *Valiant* and *Queen Elizabeth* in Alexandria, using the ingenious "Maiali" SLCs.

But there was more. In 1942, two visionary minds—Lieutenant Eugenio Wolk and Engineer Angelo Belloni—were orchestrating a plan that could have forever changed the course of submarine warfare: an attack on New York Harbor.

The plan was to be executed with surgical precision:
1. A modified ocean-going submarine, the *Da Vinci*, would transport a Caproni CA2 midget submarine, only 10 meters long and weighing 16 tons, to the U.S. coast.
2. Upon arrival at the mouth of the Hudson River, the "mother submarine" would release the CA2, from which the raiders would exit to execute the attack using preloaded explosives.
3. Moving up the river, the men would place charges on exposed ships in New York Harbor, at the heart of U.S. economic and military power.

In addition to New York, the operation's planners had also considered a strike on the port of Freetown in Sierra Leone, then a key British naval base. Four examples of the CA class, secretly built in Provaglio d'Iseo, were tested in Lake Iseo, where special hatches were added to allow Gamma operators to exit underwater. But Italy's surrender in 1943, and the simultaneous loss at sea of the Leonardo da Vinci, brought everything to a halt, leaving that dream of glory buried among classified documents.

All we can do is imagine what might have happened if the mission had gone forward. Could we really have seen a team of Italian raiders navigating the Hudson beneath the Statue of Liberty? Today, those Montecolino ruins still guard the secret of a mission that almost changed the world.

Perhaps, while traveling that road between Iseo and Pilzone, it's worth stopping to listen to the echo of a secret that nearly rewrote history.

Peace Agreements and Surrender at Montecolino?

After the Armistice, the factory became home to the Decima MAS Precision Mechanical Workshop. This marked the start of another chapter, even more cloaked in legend.

Part of the story is tied to Mussolini's final days and his attempted escape to Switzerland via Lake Como. Long story short, the famous bag Mussolini carried—rumored to contain the Churchill correspondence—was a major object of search. Within those documents was allegedly a draft agreement for a separate peace between the Italian Social Republic (RSI) and the Allies, negotiated at what would become known as the "Lake Iseo Conference."

Locals have long whispered that Montecolino promontory and the nearby villa on San Paolo Island hosted several secret meetings in November 1944.

Among those said to have attended was Sergio Nesi, a trusted officer of Junio Valerio Borghese, commander of the X^a MAS, which had taken up headquarters in the area. The meeting supposedly took place at the Decima Flottiglia MAS base on Montecolino, formerly the Caproni factory. The interpreter was said to be Borghese's wife, Russian noblewoman Daria Olsuffieff. Present were senior British officers representing Churchill and his staff, along with American officers representing Roosevelt.

On the German side, Ambassador Rahn and SS Commander in Italy General Wolff reportedly attended. Mussolini himself was absent, but his proxy was Francesco Maria Barracu, Undersecretary to the Presidency (one of those executed at Dongo), joined by General Giuseppe Violante (GNR), Commander Fausto Sestini (Repubblican Navy), and Junio Valerio Borghese (X^a MAS).

It's important to note that no official documents confirm these claims. However, history shows that meetings to discuss final surrender terms did occur—perhaps not at the highest levels, and perhaps only exploratory in nature—but they were real. In fact, one such negotiation led to Operation Sunrise on April 29, 1945, the surrender of German troops in Italy without Hitler's or Mussolini's consent.

▲▼ Montecolino base: in the arm of the lake in front of the base a Caproni 316 seaplane. Below: trials with a type 2-3-4 CA boat in the same waters of the lake. Below right: the manor house where secret meetings may have been held. And finally, a new view from above the base.

THE ADIGE–GARDA TUNNEL: BETWEEN HISTORY, WAR, AND INGENUITY

The tunnel, a monumental 10-kilometer straight structure, has its origins in an ancient need: to tame the floods of the Adige River, which had repeatedly devastated the countryside and cities—Verona in particular. After centuries of ineffective interventions, in 1926, engineer Luigi Milani revived a bold 18th-century project that envisioned using Lake Garda as a compensation basin.

The Tunnel in the Storm of War (1943–1945)
With the outbreak of the war, work on the tunnel slowed drastically, eventually halting completely after September 8, 1943, when the Germans occupied the area. The tunnel, partially flooded by then, found a new purpose: first as an air raid shelter for civilians, then as the site of a secret weapons production base. In the spring of 1944, within those cold, damp walls, Caproni transferred its aeronautical production. Roughly 1,300 workers labored to assemble engines for the feared Messerschmitt Me 262, the first operational jet fighter, as well as components for the Reich's secret weapons: the V1 flying bombs and V2 rockets designed by Wernher von Braun.

Campini–De Bernardi: The First Jet-Powered Midget Submarine
Among the many stories from that period, one stands out: the creation of a futuristic invention, the Campini–De Bernardi jet-powered midget submarine, designed by engineer Secondo Campini. Developed between the tunnel, Fort San Nicolò, and Rovereto, this assault vessel represented the technological peak of the era, a product of collaboration between Caproni and V.E.N.A.R. of Milan.
But challenges were constant: internal sabotage, deportations, and Allied bombings put production at great risk. Yet despite everything, the Adige–Garda tunnel remained a clandestine site of ingenuity and resilience, writing a little-known but fascinating chapter of Italy's wartime industrial and technological history. Today, while the waters of Lake Garda return to their deep blue, the tunnel still serves its original flood-control function, silently guarding memories that far exceed its hydraulic purpose.

The Allies Discover the Secret Project
In August 1944, through the ULTRA codebreaking system, the British intercepted a classified communication between the Kriegsmarine in Torbole and the Japanese embassy in Rome. The content was astonishing: for some time, envoys from the Imperial Japanese Navy, accompanied by Mitsubishi engineers, had settled in Merano—then under Gauleiter Franz Hofer's control—with one precise goal: to obtain the designs and know-how for the jet-powered midget submarine developed in the Adige–Garda tunnel.
Meanwhile, the project's two architects—Major Mario De Bernardi (a famous test pilot) and Engineer Secondo Campini—were split by the war's events: De Bernardi ended up in liberated Rome, while Campini remained in the RSI. It's likely that De Bernardi passed information to the Americans, especially considering he was later hired by the U.S. Defense Department to work on aircraft research.

A Prototype That Never Entered Production
Despite numerous hydrostatic tests conducted in Lake Garda, the revolutionary underwater assault craft never reached mass production. With the Allied advance in 1945, the project collapsed. Japanese delegates, surprised by partisans near Vicenza, were arrested with the submarine's blueprints in their pockets. As for the prototype itself, it vanished in the chaos of war's end: some say it was strafed by American aircraft, others claim it was seized by the U.S. 10th Mountain Division on April 30, 1945, during the occupation of the region. The truth is, nothing more was ever heard of it.

The Fate of the Adige–Garda Tunnel
The Caproni machinery, miraculously saved from destruction or deportation to Germany, remained hidden within the tunnel. After the war, the flood-control tunnel, still incomplete and flooded, was abandoned. Work resumed only in the mid-1950s and was completed in 1959. Since then, the tunnel has been activated 12 times, the most recent being on October 29, 2018.

▲▼ Base of the Adige-Garda tunnel: above, American soldiers discover the base as they walk up the lakeside promenade. Below: several period pictures of the workshops in the long tunnel, where not only the jet submarine but also components for the famous German Messerschmitt Me 262 aircraft were produced.

ASSAULT VEHICLES MODELS

The model production of many assault vehicles, submarines and other Navy equipment is the work of Italian and international companies. This is led by Italeri of Emilia and Model Vittoria of Udine. All images belong to the catalogues of the companies mentioned. Others are elaborations of various authors and modellers photographed by the author of the book in various competitions. Where possible, we dutifully mention the names of the authors.

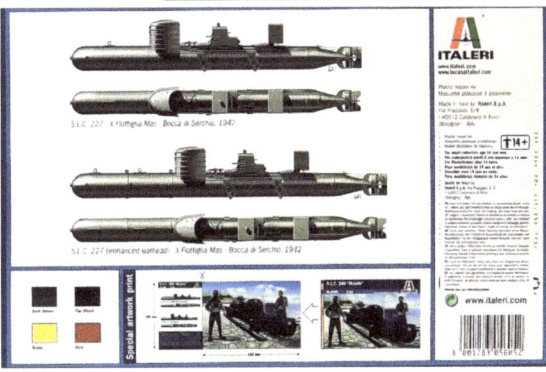

ITALIAN NAVY SPECIAL FORCES WWII

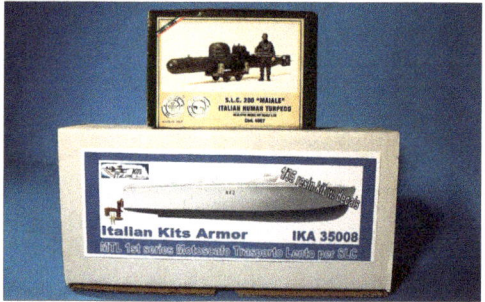

▲▼ Images of model boats and assault motorboats of the Italeri and IKA makes. The extended assault motorboat is the work of model maker Stefano Scaccianoce.

ITALIAN NAVY SPECIAL FORCES WWII

▲▼ Model images of Caproni's CA and CB class mini-submarines. Author Dino dell'Asta.

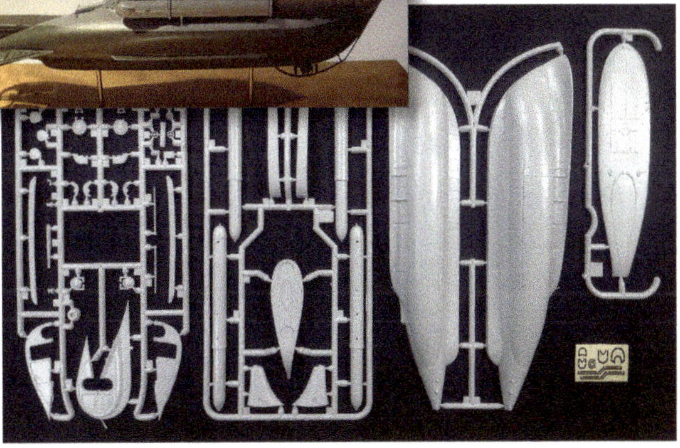

ITALIAN NAVY SPECIAL FORCES WWII

BIBLIOGRAPHY

- Crociani, Piero; Stacey, Mark; Battistelli, Pier Paolo. *Italian Navy & Air Force Elite Units & Special Forces 1940–45*. Oxford, United Kingdom: Osprey
- Virgilio Spigai. *Cento uomini contro due flotte: La storia completa dei mezzi d'assalto*. Mursia
- Carlo de Risio. *Gli affondatori. I mezzi d'assalto della Marina italiana nella II Guerra Mondiale. 1940-1945*. Editore IBN
- Luis de Sierra. *Gli assaltatori del mare. Le audaci imprese dei mezzi d'assalto delle marine militari nella Seconda guerra mondiale*. Rex Gesta
- Luciano Garibaldi e Gaspare di Sclafani. *Così affondammo la Valiant. La più grande impresa navale italiana della seconda guerra mondiale*. Lindau editore
- Giorgio Giorgierini. *Attacco dal mare. Storia dei mezzi d'assalto della Marina Italiana*. Mondadori
- Marco Romagnoli. *X flottiglia. Uniformi e armamenti della Decima MAS*. Ediz. Ritter Milano.
- AA.VV. *Decima Mas. I mezzi d'assalto della marina italiana*. Italia Editrice
- Sergio Nesi. *Decima Flottiglia nostra...: I mezzi d'assalto della Marina italiana al sud e al nord dopo l'armistizio*. Mursia
- Alessandro Turrini, Ottorino O. Miozzi e Manuel M. Minuto, *Sommergibili e mezzi d'assalto italiani (due volumi)*, Roma, Ufficio Storico Marina Militare, 2010.
- Sergio Nesi. *Scirè. Storia di un sommergibile e degli uomini che lo resero famoso*. Lo Scarabeo
- Marino Perissinotto. *Fino alla fine. Diario di guerra del Regio Sommergibile «Scirè» redatto dal Secondo Capo Segnalatore Livio Villa*. Edizioni Marvia.
- Fabio Ruberti. *Il relitto del sommergibile Scirè. Analisi storica e subacquea*. Ed.Indipendente
- Roberto Serra. *Orione 1943. L'ultima missione della Decima Flottiglia Mas*. Edizioni artestampa
- Annalisa Cramerotti, *Il mezzo d'assalto Campini – De Bernardi, Museo Storico Italiano della Guerra (a.c.)*, Annali N. 23 2015, Osiride Edizioni, Rovereto 2016.
- Achille Rastelli, *Caproni e il mare. Progetti e realizzazioni per la guerra navale di un grande gruppo industriale milanese,* Museo Aeronautica Gianni e Timina Caproni di Taliero, Milano, 1999,
- Luigi Romersa. *All'ultimo quarto di luna: Le imprese dei mezzi d'assalto*. Mursia
- Ferrucio Bravi e Emilio Bianchi. *Pagine di diario 1940-1945. Memorie di guerra e di prigionia di un operatore dei mezzi d'assalto della marina militare italiana*. Pezzini editore
- *I mezzi d'assalto Rilegatura all'americana*. UFFICIO STORICO DELLA MARINA MILITARE
- Fulvio Candia. *L'eroismo dei marinai italiani nella seconda guerra mondiale. Sommergibili, siluri umani, uomini gamma, mezzi d'assalto, mas*. Greco e Greco editore
- Gianni Bianchi. *Antonio Ramognino. L'ideatore dell'Olterra e Villa Carmela le basi avanzate della Xª Flottiglia MAS. La più efficace Spia Italiana*.
- Antonio Marceglia - *La notte di Alessandria*. Gianni Bianchi Editore
- Pino Belli - *19 Dicembre 1941 Alessandria*. Collana Posto di Combattimento. 1950
- Riccardo Furiassi. *Assaltatori gamma. La leggenda degli uomini straordinari*. Edelweiss
- Alfredo Brauzzi. *I mezzi d'assalto della marina italiana*. Rivista marittima
- Erminio Bagnasco e Marco Spertini, *I mezzi d'assalto della X Flottiglia Mas 1940-1945*, Parma, Ermanno Albertelli Editore, 1991.

PUBLISHED TITLES

TWE-038 EN

www.ingramcontent.com/pod-product-compliance
Ingram Content Group UK Ltd.
Pitfield, Milton Keynes, MK11 3LW, UK
UKHW060216240426
12048UKWH00030BB/1693